SHELTERED WITHIN HER HEART

33 Days of Preparation
for Deeper Entrustment to Mary

Joshua Elzner

This book has also been the basis of a class, which has been recorded. You are welcome to use the audio recordings as an accompaniment for your reading, to help you delve deeper into everything expressed here. You can find the recordings here:

atthewellspring.com/loving-christ-with-the-heart-of-mary

CONTENTS

WEEK 4 – THE ROSE THAT HEALS US AMONG OUR THORNS

CONCLUDING DAYS

INTRODUCTION

When the fullness of time at last came, and God's plan of salvation reached its moment of highest climax, all the energies of Divine Love became focused in a single place. God's Love is like an ocean, immense and immeasurable in its greatness, and yet, from the very beginning of time this Love has found a resting place in those who are small and needy. From the time of Adam and Eve, through Noah, Abraham, David, and the Prophets, God has been at work revealing himself to the littlest and the least, to the poor who are considered nothing in this world. Yet in them, because of the simplicity of their lives as his children, his Love is made beautifully manifest, and the immensity of his glory is made known in them. In a humble and lowly woman of Galilee, this energy of Divine Love was at last focused in utmost intensity, like the ocean being poured out into a thimble...and being contained within it!

The angel Gabriel came to the village of Nazareth, to a young virgin named Mary, and revealed to her that God was asking for her permission to be conceived as child within her womb. When she accepted this invitation, the Holy Spirit descended upon her and the Son of the Father was begotten within her. She sheltered and cherished him within her for nine months, living an interior life of love and prayer, and then she brought him forth into the world in Bethlehem. She nursed him, cared for him, mothered him, taught him, and lived at his side through the thirty years that he himself lived a life of silence and hiddenness.

Together they were "little ones" of God, poor, apparently insignificant, and counted as nothing in the eyes of the world. God came to us in the person of Jesus and united himself to us in all of our brokenness and need, sanctifying this place by his loving presence. And Mary shows us, through the virginal love with which she accepted God's invitation, how we ourselves are to receive the One who comes to us.

This descending movement of God, however, was not complete until the Son identified himself completely with us in loving compassion. After a few short years of preaching and active ministry, Jesus was arrested and condemned, tortured and killed in the most inhumane and humiliating way. There at the foot of the Cross of Crucifixion, his mother stood, united to him in a love and compassion that was stronger even than death.

He gave himself for the life of all, the Son of God, God himself, descending into our darkest place, and lifting us up in his arms. Here he loves us in the depths of our brokenness, our sin, and our shame, and precisely by loving us, he heals and transforms us. Liberating us from all that holds us bound, and pressing us close to his tender Heart, he breaks the bonds of death and the tomb, and draws us all back into the joy of his Father. And as he pours himself out as a perfect gift, Mary stands before him, receiving and reciprocating this gift of his love. As he breaks beyond the barrier of death, she is present; as he unleashes life, she is there, awaiting him in vigilant faith and hope.

Man and Woman, together united in mutual self-giving: this is what God intended for our first parents in the Garden of Eden, yet from which they turned away in sin, failing to trust in the pure love of their heavenly Father. Nonetheless, after many years of suffering—yet concealing a never-dying romance between God and his unfaithful Bride— at the tree of the Cross, this mystery is again restored. Indeed, it is brought to fulfillment in a way infinitely more beautiful than at first. In the union between Jesus and Mary each one of us, a child of the heavenly Father, is conceived and brought to birth. The beloved disciple, who stands at Mary's side and hears Jesus words, "Woman, behold your son...Behold, your Mother," is indeed standing in the place of each one of us. We are invited, like him, to receive her into our home, into our inmost heart and all that relates to us, and to surrender ourselves, also, completely into her care.

In this, she has only one desire, to fashion Jesus freely and fully within us, to draw us into Jesus, in whom we shall find the fullness of joy, the deepest truth of who we are, as well as the communion with God and with others for which our hearts were created and most deeply long.

Jesus is the one who has given Mary to us as our Mother, who has entrusted us into her maternal care, so that she may gently mother us as she mothered Jesus himself. Yes, Jesus was indeed the first person to entrust himself into the care of Mary, and he invites us to do as he has done. He invites us to imitate him, indeed, to do more than imitate him. He opens up his own Heart and his life to us entirely...to allow us to enter in. And he shares himself entirely with us, asking us to allow him to perpetuate his own mystery as the Son of Mary and the Son of the Father in our own person, to abide in the beauty of the same relationships that he lived and continues always to live.

He invites us to become, and to remain, a little child in the arms of our most tender Mother. He asks us to live with her, always at her side, entirely trusting in her, each day and each moment of our life. He asks us to walk with her to the foot of his Cross, where he so deeply yearns for our own loving compassion—a compassion that she herself helps to fashion and mature within us. In this way, truly discovering who we are as children of God, and allowing this gift to blossom within us, we also find ourselves drawn into the awesome nuptial embrace between God and the world, the intimate communion that alone satisfies the deepest longings of our heart.

Finally, from this most intimate embrace, in which, through the Virgin Mary and with her, we allow Jesus to abide in us, and we abide in him, we spontaneously bear fruit for the good of others. In other words, through our trusting acceptance of the love that God bears for us, and our loving surrender to him in return, we let ourselves be caught up into the romance ever being played out between God and the world.

This romance has found its most profound meeting-point in Mary, and from her it has spread out to all. When we draw close to her, she draws us into the intimacy that she shares with her Son, and, in him, with the Father, irradiated with the beauty and light of the Holy Spirit. Abiding in this place without ceasing, we also find ourselves transparent to the outpouring of God's light into the hearts of others, into the darkness of our world which is thirsting so deeply for the healing and saving love of God.

Our brothers and sisters yearn for God so deeply, whether they know it or not. So let us, who indeed recognize this thirst within us, surrender ourselves entirely to God through the hands of Mary, so that we may every day live more and more deeply in him, and allow him to live in us. This intimacy, which Mary wants to open up to us and to share with us, and yet which is unique to each of us as if it were ours alone, cannot but be an explosive force for the salvation of our brothers and sisters whom God yearns so passionately to draw back to himself.

+ + +

There are many books that have been written as aids in preparing for "consecration" or "entrustment" to Mary. Saint Louis de Montfort, who played such a pivotal role in awakening and promoting this movement of surrender to Jesus through Mary, has benefited many people. There are also more contemporary adaptations, further developments, such as Father Michael Gaitley's *33 Days to Morning Glory*, which summarizes and unites the teaching of other great Marian saints: Saint Maximilian Kolbe, Saint Teresa of Calcutta, and Saint John Paul II. This present book, while enriched by these approaches, nonetheless seeks to express a different word...or, more accurately, to express this same word in a different way. It is a response to the desires of a number of persons (and to the sense that there are many such persons) who want to go *deeper* in a life of entrustment to Mary, to grow ever more in intimacy with her and her Son.

Mary is the Mother of each and all of us, and she never ceases to draw near to us and work among us. She seeks to create a space within our hearts and our lives for the Love of God to pour itself out. She seeks to lead us back to the God for whom we long. On our own we struggle to make this journey, and she tries to help us along the way, just as any mother would. In her own virginal purity and maternal love she gazes upon us with a penetrating gaze, a gaze that shares in the gaze of God himself. Yet often it is precisely this gaze of God that we find most difficult to understand and to accept. The brokenness and shame of our hearts can hinder us from *allowing ourselves to be looked upon with love*. But it is precisely this gaze of love that, penetrating us and touching our woundedness, healing and transfiguring us, gives birth to the joy and gladness for which we long.

How then can we learn to let ourselves be looked upon by our loving God? We can allow Mary into our lives, she who was looked upon by God in the most intense of ways, chosen to be Daughter, Bride, and Mother of God. We can allow her to foster this receptivity within us, *she who is, above everything else, a little child of the heavenly Father*. And here she is indeed not raised up far from us, but right at our side, a little one just as we are little. She knows, more than anyone else, what it means to be a child of God, for she lived this reality herself, free from all the woundedness and dullness of sin that we experience, and also walked most intimately with the true Son of the Father, who is her Son as well.

In being looked upon with love by the Virgin Mother, as well as especially by the heavenly Father, we will find ourselves healed, freed, and transformed, and will discover that we too are beginning to look upon others with eyes of love, within the light that has first bathed us in its radiance.

This emphasis on heart-healing through relationship with Mary—this is the approach of this book, which is intended either to be an avenue for entrusting oneself to Mary for the first time, or for renewing and deepening this entrustment. It does this not by focusing on the external elements of such consecration, which can be found elsewhere (such as the historical development or devotional practices), but on seeking to lead the reader into a more intimate relationship with God through the Virgin Mary.

As was said, the reflections contained in this book are intended to facilitate the process of heart-healing, healing of the wounds we have received through original and personal sin, as well as through the other circumstances or persons in our life that have hurt and wounded us. Only in the healing encounter with the love of God will we find blossoming the sanctity for which God created us, sanctity which is nothing else than the joy of loving relationship with God and with every person.

These reflections are, thus, intended to help bring all that we are, our brokenness as well as our beauty, to Mary, who will carry us to the healing and cherishing love of the Trinity. In this way, hopefully, a deeper, more spontaneous, and more intimate relationship with Mary will develop, allowing her to free us from everything that hinders us from rejoicing in the joy of being children of God. And, of course, in her we will find ourselves abiding ever more deeply against the loving Heart of Jesus, held by him close to the Father, and sharing with them the Spirit of love who first overshadowed Mary in the beginning of this beautiful story.

6

Note:

The following reflections should be short enough for you to pray and reflect upon them each day, becoming acquainted with the main themes that they bring forth and trying to interiorize them in the presence of God. However, the content is nonetheless rich and involved, and much of it is probably new to you; therefore, please feel free to take this book at your own pace. There is no need whatsoever to follow it in a strict period of 33 Days. What is important is that you interiorize the themes which are expressed herein, and pray through them in a way that allows God to speak as he desires.

Gradually the reflections will build on one another, day after day, hopefully opening the way to a deeper interior vision of Mary's intimate relationship with us, and the "Marian" character of our own relationship with God. There will also be some reflection questions after each day, in order to prompt deeper thought and prayer.

WEEK 1

CRADLED IN THE ARMS OF LOVE

DAY 1: BORN FROM LOVE

At the beginning of these 33 days of preparation to entrust our-selves into the loving hands of Mary, we first take a step back in order, as it were, to get "a running start." For the first week, we will be prepar-ing the ground for the following three weeks; therefore, the name of Mary will not be mentioned extensively in this first week, though her spiritual presence, as you will see, shall be deeply present, permeating our reflections.

In order to understand the beautiful role of Mary in God's plan of salvation, in the life of faith of each one of us, we must first look at two things: 1) the mystery of woman herself in creation, and her role in revealing the face of Love; 2) the original experience of Adam and Eve in the Garden of Eden, and how this experience was fractured because of sin. These two are indeed deeply related to one another, for it is pre-cisely in our relationship with a woman—with our mother—that we come closest to experiencing this original purity of contact with Love that Adam and Eve knew in the Garden.

So let us begin by asking: what is our most fundamental human ex-perience, the one on which all of our other experiences of life are based? **It is the experience of being totally and unconditionally loved... indeed, of receiving one's very existence as a gift of love from another.** This is the unique mystery revealed by the *mother*, and through her, by the *father* whose gift she receives and brings forth.

The world has been born from Love and returns to Love, and it is enveloped in the arms of Love. This is particularly true for each one of us, for every unique human person created in the image and likeness of God. Despite the claims of our contemporary world, we do not enter into the world and the human community as isolated and autonomous individuals. We do not enter the world in such a way that everyone else remains "outside" of and arbitrary to us, and matters to us only insofar as we wish to let them in. Rather, we are born from the very heart of community, from within the context of the coming-together of per-sons in love. We owe our very being, our very life to other persons—to our parents. And not only that, but we awaken to self-consciousness, not from enclosed within ourselves, but precisely from the love that we receive from the outside, from the look and the smile of another.

Let us reflect for a moment on the most basic and foundational experience that each one of us has as a little child, as an infant in the arms of our mother. A little child shortly after birth has not yet awakened to a full self-consciousness, that is, to a consciousness of her own "I" as separate from the world around her and from the "You" of other persons. Of course, she lives these relationships already—as she did even in the womb—and implicitly experiences this relationality that marks her whole existence. But there comes a point when the full light of personal awareness dawns upon her, or rather awakens within her. As we said, this comes about precisely through the presence of another, through the love that she receives from another.

The mother holds her child in her arms, close to her bosom, and smiles upon her. At some point, this child, looking into the loving eyes of her mother and receiving her smile, spontaneously smiles back. What is happening here? The little child is having a profound *intuition* which proves to be the foundation for all of the experiences of the rest of her life. This is her "original experience" that sets the context for everything else that follows. What is she experiencing? In this moment of encounter, she awakens to full personal awareness, and her experience is: *You... Me... and the love between us.*

This is what the child experiences in this moment of recognition. She awakens to the beauty and mystery of the other person, of her mother, who is for her a source of love, of security, and of peace. And precisely from her recognition of the other, she becomes fully aware of herself: of her own unique "I." In a profound sense, her own "I" is a gift to her from another; she receives herself as a gift from the love of another person. Therefore, she belongs to herself only because she first belongs to another; she is her own only because she is a gift.

Further, this mutual relationship of "You" and "I" is entirely sealed with the joy of *communion*, in an intimacy that is utterly safe and secure. The child feels protected by her mother; she feels herself, indeed, to be entirely enveloped in the arms of Love, which her mother manifests and symbolizes for her. Because she experiences her own personal identity, not in isolation, but precisely in the context of loving relationship, of intimacy, she feels no need to close herself off from the other, to protect her own "individuality" from the other. Rather, she feels that she comes from communion, and thus wants to return to communion ever more deeply.

In this encounter between mother and child, the child is profoundly dependent on her mother for everything, especially at first. Nonetheless, this dependence is not a threat to the individuality of the child, but rather the very "space" in which this individuality grows and matures in safety. In a word, the little child's own unique and unrepeatable identity is not threatened by the identity of her mother. They are both distinct, and yet they are one; they are united. Indeed, it is precisely because they are two, two different persons, that they can be united in the deepest way, not by being absorbed into each other and losing their individuality, but by sharing themselves with one another, by belonging to one another in love and trust. This sharing exists at such an intimate level in the relationship between mother and child that the child even lives *within* her mother for more than nine months. Further, this living within the womb of another is not only a matter of location, for the child is dependent on her mother in every way for her own life, sustenance, and growth. The womb is the place of all-enveloping and sheltering love, the place where the vulnerable and defenseless child is protected, cared for, and allowed to grow and develop in her own unique and sacred life.

Even when the child is brought forth into the world through the labor-pains of her mother (which again is an expression of the giving and sharing of oneself), she is still dependent upon her mother. Yes, she still indeed drinks of the being and the body of her mother for a long time after birth. Here we see the beautiful interchange of persons that lies at the origin of our human experience in this world. The child receives all from her mother, from her mother's generosity and love; and the mother in turn receives from the child. First of all, her very willingness to carry her child and to bring her into the world is an act of love and generosity. Therefore, in order to *give* herself to her child, she must first be willing to *accept* the child. And she continues to accept her, and receives from her child just as the child receives from her. Often times what she receives is "morning sickness" or aches in the lower back, but on a deeper level she receives the joy of this new, precious life growing within her. She receives the child's first kicks, her movements in the womb. Then the mother receives the first encounter after birth, and the long days of care and nurture in which she is touched and enriched, challenged and transformed by this life, by this precious and beloved person, for whom she cares and gives herself.

In summary, we see in this most basic human relationship a glimpse of the deep meaning of Jesus' words: "Abide in me, and I in you" (Jn 15). The mother and child live *with*, and in a deep way, *for* one another. And because of this deep sharing, they also live *in* one another, if not physically, then spiritually, emotionally, personally. They carry one another in the heart.

You… Me… and the love between us, the love that unites us together…

Reflection Questions:

— *Even though this "original experience" is too early in my life to be explicitly remembered, do I find myself able to "reconnect" with it through prayer and reflection?*

— *What obstacles may there be in me to recognizing that I have come as a gift of love from another, and that union with others is not a threat to my individuality, but rather a help to me in being truly free and happy?*

DAY 2: IMAGE OF THE TRINITY

In yesterday's reflection, we began our journey by looking at the "foundational experience" of the little child in the arms of her mother. We said that this experience, as it were, "paves the way" for all future experiences of our life in this world. Indeed, it is meant to be a kind of interpretive key, a lens through which we can understand the meaning of our existence. What did we say that this key was? It is the unspoken intuition that all things come from Love, are enfolded in Love, and re-turn to Love…that my own life itself is cradled unceasingly in the arms of Love. It is also the intuition that *intimacy* is the deepest meaning of human life and our highest vocation, the only space in which our hearts can truly find rest. Precisely the mother, in a unique way, reveals this mystery to her child, and we will soon see how our Blessed Mother, Mary, plays an important role in giving us access to this "key" once again. But let us now try to go deeper into this foundational experience, to draw to light more of its characteristics.

In this parent-child relationship, we see not only a kind of "sanctu-ary" of love that God has preserved in the heart of his creation (where the child can receive the love so necessary for her well-being, even if the surrounding world is broken and fractured). We see even more: **we recognize that this relationship is a beautiful "image" of the Trinity— of the intimacy shared eternally by the Father and the Son in their one Spirit**. How is this? Let us try to cast our interior gaze, in faith, upon what God has revealed concerning his own inner life as Trinity. Let us try to contemplate his beauty revealed to us in Christ, and made clear through the teaching of his Church. We will see how this fulfills, in the most perfect way, what we spoke about in the previous reflection: the reality of *You*, *Me*, and the *Love* between us…and also the way in which distinct persons share together in the most perfect "We" of together-ness without losing their uniqueness, but rather find it fulfilled precisely in the intimacy that they share.

For all eternity, the Father gives himself totally to the Son; he pours out his very life and being into the Son in pure and unconditional love. And this act of total self-donation is also, simultaneously, an act of perfect acceptance, in which the Father makes himself a welcoming-space and a home for his beloved Son. The Son, for his part, welcomes this gift of the Father, in which he has his own true identity as the Son, as the One who is loved by the Father and in relationship with the Father. He knows his *"I"* before the *"You"* of the Father; and in this knowledge, in this mutual beholding, he receives the gift of himself and gives himself spontaneously and freely back to the Father. Finally, the *Love* that the Father and the Son share, the gift that passes eternally between them, is the Holy Spirit. Yes, the Spirit is the Love that binds the Father and the Son together in perfect intimacy; he is, as it were, the Kiss that they share, so intimate that their breath mingles together as one.

In the relationship between mother and child—and in all human relationships, each in their own way—this mystery of the Holy Trinity is constantly revealed and at work. We said that the mother-child relationship is a kind of "sanctuary" that God has preserved in the midst of our fallen and broken world, so that each one of us will receive the foundational experience on which the rest of our lives can be built and from which they can blossom. This experience is the experience of coming as a gift from the love of another. It is also an experience of coming from communion, being enveloped in communion, and growing into communion. One's own individuality, one's own personal identity, is not opposed to union with the other, to belonging to the community, but rather matures precisely within it—within the trust-filled sharing of persons in love.

From this space of intimate relationship, as the child grows, her self-awareness deepens. She becomes more conscious of her "I" and lives it with greater deliberateness. And this is an entirely good thing. Communion is not the loss of individuality in a mass of "togetherness," but the fully conscious, fully free sharing of persons with one another in love. This allows them to be aware both of the "I" and the "You," and also of the "We" that their unity makes possible. This living of the "I" and "You" together, their living in one another, and their sharing a common experience of intimacy: this is the truest and deepest joy that the human heart can experience. Indeed, it is precisely *this* breathtaking intimacy for which we have been created.

It is also important to note that this human relationship bears in itself a mystery greater than itself. When the child awakens to the love of her mother, when she experiences her own self enfolded in the shelter of love, she has an intuition that *the deepest truth of reality itself is Love.* She connects in her mind and her heart the reality of **Love** and the reality of **Being**. What exists is good and beautiful because it comes from Love, returns to Love, and remains enveloped in Love. Yes, it is all an expression of Love, an "outpouring" of Love's abundant generosity. (Here the statement of God to Moses—I AM HE WHO IS—is spontaneously glimpsed to be I AM HE WHO IS LOVE.) Of course, this intuition is not some kind of intellectual theory or a concept in the child's mind. Rather, it is, as we have said, the "original experience" and the foundational awareness—at the wellspring of all thought, emotion, and willing—from which the rest of human life is meant to mature and blossom.

This also means that the child is naturally and spontaneously a believer in God. No person is naturally an atheist. Denial of God's existence is profoundly contrary to nature and the aspirations of the human heart. It is, rather, caused by human brokenness and sin, a rupture where there was meant to be unity, blindness where there was meant to be vision. But in the experience of love and communion, the human heart spontaneously expands to an awareness of God. It expands from an experience of love (small "l") to a recognition of Love (capital "L"). It is only necessary for the parents of the child to foster this, to protect it, and through their words, their example, and their instruction, to help the child grow up into a conscious, mature, and free relationship with God.

This too is perhaps the best way to explain the mystery of the Trinity, not as an abstract idea, but rather as it really is: *a Family of Persons joined together in Love.* In this way a door is opened for an intimate relationship with the Father, Son, and Holy Spirit to grow and deepen. Our most intimate human experiences, in other words, unveil for us—however little—a glimpse of the immense Beauty of the Trinity, who is for all eternity a Community of Persons existing in perfect intimacy with one another. Just as the mother and child belong to another another intimately, being united together in a single love that "knits" their hearts together, so this is even more true of the Father, Son, and Holy Spirit. The very beauty of human intimacy in this world was deliberately made by God as an "image" of his own Divine Life, and it awakens in our hearts the longing to return to this Life. For only in the sheltering embrace of the Trinity can our hearts, touched by human intimacy but thirsting for more, at last find enduring rest.

Reflection Questions:

— What is my response to hearing that communion is an experience of "You" and "I" coming together in the "We" of intimacy? Does this awaken my desire, or does it cause me fear?

— Do I see the world as an expression of God's perfect creative Love, or do I see it (as our contemporary secular world does) as a mere product of random chance that has no inherent meaning? Or, if I do believe in God's Love, does my attitude toward life reflect this belief?

— Do I feel a "connection" with the mystery of the Trinity as described here? If so, can I ask the Father, Son, and Holy Spirit to deepen this revelation? If not, can I invite the divine Persons to reveal themselves to me and give me a glimpse of their love and their mystery?

DAY 3: THE FRACTURE OF SIN

We said in the previous reflection that the relationship between mother and child is a sanctuary that God has preserved in the midst of creation. In this space God provides a safe place in which we can grow; he also gives us a foundational intuition of the mystery of Love and of our deepest vocation to intimacy. Finally, as we said, this encounter of love is an image of the very inner life of the Trinity itself.

From this sacred space of the relationship with her mother, the child will naturally grow into a healthy sense of her own individuality and into loving and trust-filled relationships with others. However, as we know, there are also many things that militate against this natural development. The world we live in is profoundly broken, and what God has joined together has been rent asunder by human sin. We need to think only of the tragedy of abortion, in which the womb that was meant to shelter becomes the most unsafe place. Or we think of the wounds that are so often left by adoption—which in itself is a gift of loving acceptance and desire by the adoptive parents, but which takes time to be understood by the adopted child, who often has the ingrained sense that one has been rejected by one's biological parents and is therefore unwanted. In a word, healing and liberation comes when the face of Love and its sheltering embrace is rediscovered as stronger even than the limitations and failures of one's parents. We think also of neglect or abuse. If you are someone who has suffered from any of these, you have probably found the above meditations very difficult. I only ask you to persevere...for there is a powerful and beautiful answer.

God created us out of the abundance of his pure love and generosity; he fashioned us to be as a little child in his arms, receiving and reciprocating his smile, his look, his embrace. We are born from the communion of the Trinity's life and invited to return at last into the fullness of the Trinity's perfect embrace...into the beauty of the communion shared eternally by the Father, Son, and Holy Spirit. However, from the first sin of Adam and Eve until now, the human heart has been tempted to tear apart the inseparable union between "You" and "I." It has been tempted to refuse to be dependent on Another, to receive oneself as a gift from Another, to belong to Another in vulnerability and love.

The temptation of the serpent was precisely this, wasn't it? Let us read the account:

> Now the serpent was more subtle than any other wild creature that the LORD God had made. He said to the woman, "Did God say, 'You shall not eat of any tree of the garden'?" And the woman said to the serpent, "We may eat of the fruit of the trees of the garden; but God said, 'You shall not eat of the fruit of the tree which is in the midst of the garden, neither shall you touch it, lest you die.'" But the serpent said to the woman, "You will not die. For God knows that when you eat of it your eyes will be opened, and you will be like God, knowing good and evil." So when the woman saw that the tree was good for food, and that it was a delight to the eyes, and that the tree was to be desired to make one wise, she took of its fruit and ate; and she also gave some to her husband, and he ate. Then the eyes of both were opened, and they knew that they were naked; and they sewed fig leaves together and made themselves aprons. And they heard the sound of the LORD God walking in the garden in the cool of the day, and the man and his wife hid themselves from the presence of the LORD God among the trees of the garden. But the LORD God called to the man, and said to him, "Where are you?" And he said, "I heard the sound of you in the garden, and I was afraid, because I was naked; and I hid myself." (Genesis 3:1-10)

The serpent tricked Adam and Eve into believing that they were not safe and sheltered in God's love, that they were not loved and desired for their own sake. Rather, he deceived them into believing that God was withholding things from them, jealous of his own "prerogatives." He also insinuated that God was a Taskmaster who imposed arbitrary burdens in order to enslave his creatures to himself. He made them think that the communion that enfolded them, the all-enveloping embrace of the Father, was *constricting* them from being their true selves, and that in order to be free and "mature" they needed to rebel and go their own way. Rather than abiding in childlike playfulness within the enveloping security of the Father's love, in the joy and peace of being infinitely and unconditionally loved, they wanted to be in "control" and to go their own way. In this desire for a false autonomy, **they were tempted to create from within themselves what could only come as a gift from the outside.**

In truth, *they* were a gift from Another, and in simply accepting this gift they had everything else as well. The Father's Love enfolded and protected them, and as long as they consented to remain rooted in this Love, to remain always within this Love, they could exist and blossom fully in their own unique personal existence. Here "You" and "I" and "We" would be profoundly united, creating together a beautiful harmony of love and relationship: the intimacy for which the human heart was created and in which alone it can be at rest! Each human person would be united to God, the loving Father, as his precious child. And from this place of communion with God, they would also be able to relate to other human persons in freedom, confidence, and joy—since all of their relationships would spring from the Father's Love within them and remain encompassed within this Love. In other words, because all would abide in the bosom of the Father, they would be able to share themselves with one another too, being united profoundly within the intimacy that God's cradling Love makes possible.

But, as we know, Adam and Eve turned away... They chose the path of isolation rather than the path of communion. They refused to belong to Another—to the One who was the very Source of their existence and their only true Home. They refused to be vulnerable before the gift of his love, and to give themselves to him, and to one another, in return. Rather, they grasped the gift as their own possession and turned it away from the Giver. They wanted to master it, to make it merely their own (even though it *was* their own, precisely as his gift!). They wanted to bring forth from within themselves the fulfillment of their desires—desires which only unceasing acceptance of God's free gift can satisfy.

And now the whole history of our world, and every human life, is marked by the rupture that this first sin caused, and which is perpetuated in every sin committed since. Now we see that, corresponding to the "original experience" of enveloping Love, there is an "original rupture" which seeks to cut off the human heart from this Love, to close it in upon itself. Rather than expanding on the touch of Love, being wide-open and vulnerable in trusting acceptance and reciprocal surrender, the heart is tempted to collapse into narrowness in fear and shame, crying out with Adam: "I was afraid, because I was naked, so I hid myself." Every sin, indeed, can be understood as a way of "hiding from the Lord God among the trees of the garden." A way of seeking to cover over one's vulnerability with partial and fading things. A way of seeking fulfillment in what cannot satisfy.

We saw earlier that, in her experience of her mother's love, the little child spontaneously desires to receive this love ever more deeply and to give herself back in return. The same was true of Adam and Eve before the fall—in relationship with their loving Father. But after sin, the very face of Love was fractured for them, since they could no longer see, their trust in the goodness of the Father having died in their hearts. Because of this, the ardent and life-giving *desire* that springs spontaneously from loving encounter—from that shared smile of recognition —is submerged under the *fear* of being unsafe, unsheltered, and unloved. **The human person now begins to live out of fear rather than out of desire.** He or she sees life, vulnerable human relationships, and the commands of God, no longer as a liberating gift, as a pure expression of Love's generosity, but as an external and arbitrary burden, constricting the heart. One thinks that one must now "measure up" and attain through one's own efforts to what was meant only to be *a pure gift,* received, interiorized, and lived in joyful freedom.

Rather than living *from* Love, *within* Love, and ever deeper *into* Love, the person now feels that it is necessary to live *toward* Love…a Love that is inaccessible and absent and can only be found at the end of a long and lonely journey. This, of course, is a lie. God's Love is just as present to us as it has always been; it still envelops us entirely on all sides; it still penetrates every fiber of our being. But we have become closed to its presence, and turned in upon ourselves. The living relationship that was meant to be ours with God has been ruptured by sin, by false independence, by fear. Our hearts have collapsed in upon themselves, and we are tempted clothe ourselves with whatever we can find to hide our nakedness…since we are afraid to open ourselves to vulnerability, uncertain of whether or not authentic Love will be there to receive and shelter us.

Reflection Questions:

— *In what ways is my own image of the heavenly Father distorted? Do I see him as a Taskmaster rather than a Father, as an angry and judgmental God rather than the "Father of mercies and God of all consolation"?*

— *In what ways do I find myself "hiding among the trees of the garden" and concealing my vulnerability from the face of God? Why do I do this?*

— *How can I re-open myself to receiving the free gift of his love again, when I am tempted to turn away? How can I let him hold me in his loving arms, as the little beloved child that I am?*

DAY 4: RE-OPENING TO THE GIFT OF LOVE

In the last reflection, we saw the tension that exists, in our fallen world, between the beauty of Love inviting us into the fullness of relationship, and the disorder of possessiveness and fear which inclines us to close ourselves off from others. Let us go deeper here, to see how this turning away in sin and false independence is precisely a loss of *gratitude* and the spirit of *playfulness*, a loss of the joy of knowing oneself to be enfolded in the love and care of another—of God himself. It is also the loss of the confidence that allows us to open ourselves, trustingly and vulnerably, to the love and gift coming to us from the outside. After noting this, we will begin to speak about the path of healing that we are invited to walk: reopening the wounds of our hearts to the healing touch of Love once again.

We saw that, upon encountering the gaze and the smile of her mother, the child spontaneously smiles back. And as she grows, this smile matures into other, more conscious, ways of expressing love. For example, she begins to want to give kisses. Even later, she wants to help her mother in any way she can—by "helping" her cook, or clean, or fold laundry. And above all she wants to *play* with her mother and in her mother's presence. Indeed, her very "helping" is but an expression of her playful attitude, and she does not at first experience it as a form of "work." Her confidence and security within all-enveloping love allows her to be carefree, relaxed, and playful. Play, indeed, is the highest expression of human activity, the ultimate "way of being" for which we were created by God. This is because work is a means to an end, and something often undertaken out of necessity, a task in service of something else. But play is its own end and is done for its own sake, a simple exuberant expression of the gratuity of existence...that is, its "unnecessary" goodness and beauty. Indeed, it is simply the expression of our joyful and trusting acceptance of life, of the gift of love, and the surrender of ourselves to its radiant mystery.

What happens, however, whenever the child experiences neglect or abuse, or a fracturing of this "original experience" that we have spoken about? This is a tragedy, which attacks the very foundational intuition of human existence—but it can be healed. In the seamless fabric of the child's experience of love there is a tear, an ugly rip. Her original experience of love is now threatened by the original rupture of sin and evil. Even without experiences of severe neglect or abuse, in the life of every one of us this original rupture becomes present. This is not only because our world is broken, and our experience of love and shelter is always in some degree imperfect. It is also because within our own hearts, due to original sin, we bear the original rupture. This rupture is manifested in what the Church calls "concupiscence," or the disordered desires to close in upon oneself in isolation, in false independence, and to grasp rather than receiving and living in complete openness.

The whole of our life, we can say, is a matter of healing the original rupture and returning to the original experience—and, indeed, as we will see, of surrendering to the Love that we first glimpsed in our original experience, so as to be carried into the final consummation of this experience in the arms of Divine Love that awaits us at the end of time. Our life and healing is a matter of reopening the closed heart to the openness of love once again—reopening the heart to receive anew the gift of life, the gift of oneself, and the gift of love from another… and ultimately and definitively, from God. Further, when the gift of love is received, it bears within itself the reciprocal gift. In other words, when we truly know ourselves to be loved, we spontaneously yearn to love in return, to surrender ourselves totally to the one who loves us.

But the original rupture has cut off this desire to give ourselves away in love; this is something that has been submerged under a swamp of fear and distrust. But this desire remains present nonetheless, buried under all of own wounds, our sins, our shame. Indeed, every fear indeed conceals within itself a deeper desire. Every fear is only a desire that has not found authentic expression, but rather has been repressed by hesitancy and by withdrawal from vulnerability. We can, in fact, never cease to desire love and intimacy. This is true not only because of our implicit "memory" of our original experience of love and communion in the arms of our mother, but even more fundamentally, *because of our "memory" of being created by God out of love*. This is, we could say, the "memory prior to every memory." **Each one of us has, as it were, the "fingerprint" of God impressed upon our inmost heart. This is the most fundamental "original experience" that goes even deeper than our** earliest encounter with another human being.

This "fingerprint" is, as it were, our memory of being created in God's image and likeness...being created from the bosom of his own love and communion, and in order to share in this communion. It is as if God has pressed us to his Heart at the first moment of our creation, and has indeed created us precisely through this gentle touch against his pulsating Heart, overflowing with love. Therefore, perhaps it would be better to speak of God's "heart-print." Our very innermost being bears his seal, the mark of his own unconditional and total love, and the beauty of his own Being impressed uniquely upon us...and this is something we can never erase or destroy.

Therefore we long...we yearn...we thirst...we desire... We desire to return into the arms of this Love, to experience the understanding, acceptance, shelter, and protection of the One who created us from himself and for himself.

What does all of this mean for our healing, for our passage from rupture to unity, from fear to desire, from isolation to love? First of all, it means that healing cannot come merely from within ourselves, through our own effort. Rather, we must receive the gift of love from another—from other human persons, but above all from God himself. Only in letting ourselves be loved, in welcoming the gift, can our hearts reopen and expand into the joy of love and communion again. Yes, full healing and transformation can ultimately occur only through relationship with God himself—a relationship which safeguards and enfolds all of our human relationships, but also goes much deeper. God's Love goes into the space in our inmost heart that no human hand can touch, but which has been touched by God at the very beginning, and is unceasingly cradled by him still.

We cannot heal ourselves, and yet, nonetheless, there is something we *can* do, and it takes courage. First of all, it is simply to be willing **to let ourselves be loved**. It is to open our hearts to vulnerability again, to heart-to-heart encounter, to sharing the things we want to hide, so that they can be touched and healed by love.

And within this context we can name our fears, acknowledge what closes our hearts in upon themselves, recognize that barriers we build to protect ourselves—and **open these fears to God and to others who can love us in them and through them**. But not only can we acknowledge our fears and interior obstacles, but we can look deeper: to the desire hidden underneath our fear. As we said, every fear conceals a deeper desire. The very fear of being unloved conceals the desire for love. The very fear of vulnerability hides the desire for vulnerability. The very fear of sharing oneself with another conceals precisely the desire to share oneself with someone who will understand, accept, and unconditionally love you in your unique mystery. And the fear of giving oneself away, of belong to another, conceals, mysteriously, the desire to truly become a gift to another, to commit oneself lovingly to another.

Therefore, when we open up the fears of our hearts, naming them and sharing them with the One who loves us, we can allow him to lead us to **get in touch with our deepest and most authentic desires**. It is then that the question of Christ can resound in our soul: "What do you desire?" We return from "exile" into the authentic truth of our being once again, and we recognize that we are thirsting for love, yearning for intimacy. And here God offers himself to us as the One who alone can quench our thirst and satisfy our desire…by drawing us back into the shelter of his perfect Love and everlasting intimacy.

Reflection Questions:

– If I struggle to get in touch with the love that I experienced from my parents in the earliest years of my life (or if in some way I was robbed of this experience), can I "trace my way back" even further, to the loving touch of God that has brought me into existence…and which still enfolds me at every moment?

– Do I have the courage to face and name my fears? Can I open them to the healing touch of God, and perhaps to another person whom I trust?

– Am I in touch with my deepest desires, my desires for love and intimacy? What ways are these desires expressed in my life?

DAY 5: TO GIVE MYSELF AWAY IN LOVE

We said in yesterday's reflection that every fear conceals in itself a deeper desire that is seeking to find authentic expression. Because of original sin, and because of the wounds that we have received in our own individual lives, we have a tendency to live motivated by fear rather than by desire. Indeed, sometimes we are afraid to name our desires, to come to terms with them, to allow them to express themselves. We are often afraid to desire. This is because we fear that such desires will never find authentic fulfillment, but only intensify our sense of emptiness when we realize that there is no object that can satisfy them. Or we feel guilty for having such desires, because the face of Love was obscured for us by a relationship with our parents (or others) that was primarily about "obligations" and "rules" that we were not led to understand as simply expressions of love. Perhaps we even felt that their love for us was conditional, that we had to "measure up" to be worthy of their love and approval, rather than experiencing that their love was the *prior gift* from which the rest of our life, in freedom, could flow.

This fractured experience of human love, also, corresponds with innate tendencies within the fallen human heart, in which we spontaneously project onto God, our loving Father, an image which is not true: the image of an arbitrary Taskmaster or Lord whose love is conditional upon our "perfect performance." This kind of vision of God— which as we saw is the very lie of the tempter in the Garden of Eden —leads us to repress our desires for love and intimacy under an attitude primarily motivated by fear. Yet these very desires are what fuel the fear! I yearn for unconditional love, for enduring intimacy, and yet I fear that I am not worthy of this, and so I must do all I can do *make myself* worthy. Or I even fear the vulnerability of seeking love and relationship, because I am afraid of being hurt or let-down, and so close myself off into the "safety" of my own locked and caged-up heart.

In both cases, I fail to receive my desires themselves as gifts from another, as signs and promises of the fulfillment for which I was made…as gifts corresponding with the deepest meaning of my own life and with the authentic desires of the One who gives me this life. But the truth is this: the only ultimate reason that God created me was precisely *for the sake of love and intimacy!* He made me for the sake of deep and abiding intimacy with him…such that I am always cradled in his innermost embrace, sheltered in his tender love for me. And, secondarily, he also made me for the sake of communion with my brothers and sisters, a communion made possible precisely within the all-enfolding Love of God that binds us together and allows us to be open to one another in confidence and mutual understanding.

All of this being said, it is precisely my deepest and most authentic desires—for love, for intimacy, for mutual understanding, for the experience of being cherished, accepted, reverenced, and held!—that reveal the deepest truth of who I am. Indeed, they open the door for me to experience *the way in which God himself sees me, the authentic truth of who I am in his loving eyes.* By getting in touch with these desires, therefore, I can open these desires to his healing and loving gaze, and find myself gradually set free by the gift of his total and unconditional love.

Let us go more deeply into this by looking again at the dichotomy between fear and desire. We were saying earlier that fear is felt as a heavy external obligation, a burden arbitrarily placed on our shoulders. This is because the awareness of love is lost, and we no longer see our life, and the intentions of God concerning us, as a loving gift. We are therefore tempted to spend our life either running away from obligation, or embracing it as a lifeless burden. How do we get beyond this dilemma? Part of it is to recognize that *obligation* is not truly proper to fear, but rather to *love,* that it finds its meaning and purpose not in fear but in love. In our culture, of course, this is difficult to see, for we live in a world that is afraid of obligation, afraid of any commitment that comes from the outside which could hinder our so-called "autonomy." However, the deeper truth of the matter is that obligation springs spontaneously from love and desire. In other words, obligation is not meant to be a matter of fear and external necessity, but rather something that arises from the depths of our own heart, awakened to love in response to the gift of the other.

In short, love desires to oblige itself. This is because, in receiving love from another, the heart desires spontaneously to give itself back—totally and forever. Therefore love willingly embraces obligation—and obliges itself to the other. This is clear in the very word obligation (*ob-*

ligo) which means "to bind" oneself. We see this, for example, in the case of love between man and woman. When their love is mature, they want to bind themselves to one another in a lifelong commitment, because they want their union, their self-giving, their intimacy to endure forever and to grow to its full flowering. Also, touched by the beauty and goodness of the other, of the one whom they love, they yearn to bring joy to the other person and to serve with all their heart the full flowering of the other person in happiness, freedom, and joy. This, too, leads to a profound movement of "binding" oneself to another—both in intimacy and in pursuit of the other's good—which is really simply the handing over of oneself to another.

Do our hearts pull back in fear before such a radical surrender into the hands of another? Surely no human person is capable of receiving such a surrender? This is correct. In truth, no created being is capable of receiving such a gift in its fullness. Only in God can we truly make such an absolute surrender, a complete and trusting abandonment of ourselves into his loving hands. But when we give ourselves to God, then we are opened also to give ourselves to *God in the other*, and to *the other in God*. In this way, even our surrender to other human persons can be, in a way, absolute, because it rests in God and not in the other alone. Further, it springs from the wellspring of God's own love and our reciprocal love for God, which encompasses in itself our particular relationships with other persons.

But how can we begin to restore our lost confidence in God's love, in his sheltering embrace that gives us the confidence and the desire to surrender ourselves in such a way? How can we begin anew to experience the all-enveloping arms of Love—the shelter, the care, the tenderness, the protection of Love—which alone can awaken and sustain our loving response?

We said that in the previous reflection that it is necessary to receive love from the outside, to receive the gift of healing through the love of another. But ultimately no human person, however necessary and important they are in our path of healing, and however mature and constant their love is, can fully bring us the love we seek. This is because we thirst for a Love that is infinite and eternal; a Love that is boundless; a Love that envelops us entirely in itself and penetrates our entire being; a Love that knows everything about us and still cherishes us as sacred and beautiful, that indeed is the very source and safeguard of our beauty, our value, and our unique mystery.

In our next reflection we will see how God comes to minister to us precisely in this deep need for absolute Love...how he touches us in our very fear and brokenness in order to re-open us to his gift. Yes, we will begin to see how he restores to us our experience of Love, which has become fractured, and thus leads us back into the childlike confidence that we have lost. And, at last, we will be able to immerse ourselves in contemplation of the mystery of Mary and the irreplaceable role that she plays in this process. Then all of these "preparatory" reflections will be seen in the proper light—as they are irradiated by the beauty of that woman who is cradled totally in the arms of Love, and who opens herself to us from within this Love, so as to draw us to share in her own intimacy with God.

Reflection Questions:

− *Do I see how "obligation" springs forth from gratitude and love? Do I see how it is a response to the beauty of another person, and expresses the desire to give myself to them totally?*

− *Am I afraid of this kind of commitment, this "binding" of myself in love? If so, why? Am I afraid only in relation to other human persons, or also before God?*

− *Can I see in myself the desire for love and intimacy, and how this is the expression of a thirst for total and permanent belonging to God...the thirst to be surrendered into the arms of his Love so totally that nothing can take me away from this place?*

DAY 6: IN THE BOSOM OF PERFECT LOVE

We can at last come full circle in our reflections. We spoke of the original experience of a child in her mother's arms, and how this is an image of the mystery of the Trinity. It is a glimpse of our ultimate destiny and an invitation to live from love, within love, and for love—to find ourselves and our happiness within the all-enveloping embrace of love and communion. But this primal experience of being held in the bosom of our mother, in the bosom of love, is fractured in so many ways in this world. How can it be restored, definitively and fully—not by a broken and limited human heart, but by Love himself?

Saint John writes in the beginning of his Gospel: "No one has ever seen God; the only-begotten Son, who is in the bosom of the Father, he has made him known" (Jn 1:18). Yes, here we have the answer. This verse, after our reflections, jumps out to us with a new and profound meaning. The Son, resting and playing eternally in the bosom of his Father, in the shelter and joy of his Love, comes into our world as a man among us. He is born of a human mother; he grows in human maturity. **He experiences, with us and for us, our own original experience, not only in the heart of his divine life in the Trinity, but as an infant in his mother's arms.**

He has the same intuition of Love as we do, and yet this is but the transposition of his eternal experience as the beloved Son of the Father into time…into a human mind and heart. In other words, when his human consciousness awakens to the mystery of Love, which he first encounters in the loving face of Mary, he immediately recognizes it as the all-enveloping Love of his heavenly Father. Further, as he awakens to self-consciousness, he knows who he is: *the beloved Son of such a loving Father*. Therefore, his being cradled in the arms of his mother is but an expression of his being cradled forever in the arms of his heavenly Father. Here the "image" and the "Reality," human love and Trinitarian Love, meet and intersect in the most profound way. Here Love himself is held in the arms of Love, and mediating this encounter between Love and Love, between Father and Son, is a humble woman, the Blessed Virgin Mary.

By coming to us in this awesome way, Jesus not only experiences our own humanity, our own life experience, but he does so precisely so that he can journey with us through everything. He becomes our Friend and Companion through every stage of our life, and in every experience—those full of beauty and light, and those full of sorrow and darkness. Further, he loves us in the place where we find ourselves—in the place where he unites himself to us—in the midst of our brokenness, our fear, our sin.

He loves us as the One who knows himself to be infinitely loved by the Father, who rests always in his Love, and who speaks and acts only from and within this Love. He loves us as the One who is utterly secure in the love of his Father. "The Father has not left me alone, for I always do what is pleasing to him… As the Father has loved me, so have I loved you; abide in my love" (Jn 8:29; 15:9). Precisely by loving us in this way, Jesus can re-open our own hearts to recognize the face of the Father, and, yes...to recognize that we too are his beloved children. Jesus loves us as the beloved Son, and so reveals to us that we have been created to be beloved children of the Father, to be sheltered in the cradling arms of his Love forever. Christ takes us up, in our fear, in our pain, in our hope, into his own loving embrace, and he holds us close to his compassionate Heart.

Yes, this movement of his love for us reaches its climax in the mystery of his Cross and Resurrection. From the depths of his own unbreakable intimacy with the Father, and his complete openness in love and trust, he pierces into the narrowness of our fear and isolation, our suffering, our loneliness, our pain—in order to break it open again from the inside. He grants us to experience anew this "original experience" that has been so threatened, so broken by the rupture of sin and evil. And yet we experience it, this all-enveloping Love, in an infinitely deeper and stronger way than ever before. **For now Love has come to us in the very depths of our brokenness, our darkness, our fear, our isolation, and has enveloped us in his embrace.**

In this way he reopens our heart to welcome his tender and generous gift. He enables us to recognize, by looking into his tender gaze upon us, the depths of his love for us, and our own unique identity in his eyes. And, touched by this Love, this breathtaking Love revealed in the Heart of Jesus Crucified, we can allow ourselves to surrender, to be taken up by the movement of Love that sweeps us up in its ardent desire to unite us to itself.

We can be carried, beyond the barriers of fear, beyond the boundaries of sin, suffering, and death, into the everlasting and unbreakable light and joy of the Resurrection. Here there is only love, only the intimacy of hearts bound together in perfect communion through the vulnerability of their mutual acceptance and self-giving. Yes, the Risen Jesus carries us every day of our lives—if only we allow him to carry us —through the passion of this world and into the endless joy of the next. Indeed, he implants the seeds of hope, joy, and freedom—of deep and abiding intimacy—into our hearts and our lives even here and now in this world.

He is already close to us, already holding us. And in this closeness, he carries us unceasingly, moment by moment, toward the consummation that awaits us in the new creation. There we will be immersed forever, with him, in the tender bosom of the Father. We will rest and play, as beloved children within the beloved Son, within the all-enveloping embrace of perfect Love. We will breathe with the Father and the Son their single breath, their Spirit, of endless and eternal joy.

Reflection Questions:

– *Do I understand what is being said concerning Jesus' encounter with the Love of his Father being mediated through the love of Mary, his mother? If not, can I re-read and reflect on this section?*

– *If Mary was able to reveal the love of God to the very Son of God, then she can also reveal it to me. Indeed, her very maternal tenderness and closeness to us can help us confidently approach the Father through her. Can I ask Mary to reveal to me how much God loves me?*

– *If Jesus has really entered into the darkest, most painful, and most shame-filled places of my life, then here he can shelter me in his Love. Is there a place in my life where I have not yet acknowledged his presence? Can I invite him into that place now?*

DAY 7: THE GAZE OF LOVE

We have seen that even the Son of God himself chose to have a human mother, to experience love through the look, the smile, and the care of a woman. Mary is thus caught up, irreversibly, into the divine plan of salvation. In a way she stands at its very heart, where God's immense love meets the yearning of humanity, and the two become united in her womb.

Mary gazes upon each one of us with an intimate and tender love, and she wants us to experience this gaze. Just as the look of any mother, this gaze is life-giving; it is a look of radical acceptance, of tender affirmation, of selfless gift, and of spontaneous joy. Indeed, it is a gaze that acts as a kind of "womb" for our wounded and fearful hearts. In other words, her gaze is a safe place where we can open ourselves again, through her, to God's all-enveloping Love, letting ourselves be re-born into freedom and joy.

This is because her gaze of love unveils the deep truth of our identity in the eyes of God, an identity of which we may not be aware. My identity does not come from my activities or achievements, my desires or experiences, or even my personality. It is something deeper than all of this. It is the very gift of who I am in my inmost being. In a profound way, I am God's gaze of love upon me. **What God sees as he gazes upon me is the simple truth of who I am: the very reality of his love for me.**

As John Paul II has said:

> We are not the sum of our weaknesses and failures; we are the sum of the Father's love for us and our real capacity to become the image of his Son.

We can be tempted to see our unique personal beauty through the lens of our weaknesses and failures, and thus to struggle to see it at all. But on the other hand, we are invited to see ourselves as God sees us, and this means to see our weaknesses and failures through the light of our beauty—the beauty that the heavenly Father sees when he looks lovingly upon us and which is his gift to us. This deep and unspeakable beauty, unique and unrepeatable in the heart of each person, is the deepest and most authentic truth of who we are.

Because of wounds, fears, and sins, however, we find ourselves "out of touch" with this reality of who we really are. But it remains true nonetheless, in the inmost core of our being…at the deepest center of our personality in which we are in direct contact with God. This place in the core of our being, which the Bible calls the "heart," is that reality that we refer to when we say "I." It is the place from which we live, the deepest origin of our thoughts, desires, and decisions, and the endpoint of every experience. We ourselves cannot define or adequately explain it, or even experience it, for it is fully known to God alone. As the Psalmist says: "O Lord, have you searched me and known me… For you formed my inward being, you knitted me together in my mother's womb" (Ps 139:1, 13). And as Saint Augustine so beautifully expressed to God: "You are more interior to me than my inmost self, and also higher than my highest being."

The center of our heart has been called the "virgin-point," because this place is an interior sanctuary deeper than any human hand, any human word, any human act can touch. It is something that cannot be taken away, but is sheltered by the loving hand of God himself. Indeed, our heart is deeply oriented toward relationship with God and can find rest only in profound intimacy with him.

Mary, in a very special way, can help us to return to this place. She does this through her own maternal gaze—which simply reveals the paternal gaze of our heavenly Father—since her motherhood is but a transparent reflection of God's own immense love, which is the very source of all created fatherhood and motherhood. Indeed, she can gaze on us in this way because she herself, first of all, lives from this sacred place in the center of her own being, at the core of her identity as God's beloved child.

From this space, which she never leaves, she opens herself to us and loves us as she has been loved by God. She welcomes us into her motherly heart and fosters us through her gentle love, preparing us to encounter our loving Father himself in the fullness of his infinite Tenderness.

This is the reality that we want to begin immersing ourselves in during the coming week. Before looking in depth at Mary's spiritual motherhood, there are a few other things we want to try to see in Mary first.

In a word, we cannot understand Mary if we see in her only the role of *mother*, for she is much more than this. Her motherhood is the expression of a yet deeper identity: namely, the identity of *childhood*, and also the blossoming love of a *spouse*. These, however, are themselves expressions of her closeness to us, since we too have been created for the same reason; they reveal in a very pointed way the truth of our own identity before God, and thus the intimate relationship he desires to mature throughout our life as it unfolds within his enveloping Love.

In being child and spouse, Mary helps us therefore, not only by her role of mediation between God and us (her motherhood), but also by being the first and most perfect disciple of her Son. In a word, *she allows herself to be the Father's beloved child, and also a spouse who opens herself to the immense love of the heavenly Bridegroom; it is precisely in this relationship of profound intimacy that her motherhood also blossoms.*

Therefore, in Mary we discern the contours of the three most fundamental relationships of our human existence, into which each one of us also finds ourselves invited. In this she opens the way for us to healing and transformation in God's Love, by opening the very "space" in which our own response to God's Love and his invitation unfolds.

Reflection Questions:

— *Do I find myself capable of "looking into God's loving gaze upon me"? Or am I held back by shame, discouragement, or some other obstacle? What about with Mary, can I look into her motherly eyes?*

— *Do I feel like I am in touch with my heart, with this "virgin-point" within me that is thirsting ardently for God? Can I try to get more deeply in touch with it by praying silently and trying to "collect" myself in my interior being as it reaches out toward God?*

— *Do these three primary relationships (of being child, spouse, and parent, both physically and spiritually) resonate with me as being foundational for my own life? Which one attracts me the most? Which one do I struggle with the most?*

WEEK 2

DAUGHTER, BRIDE, AND MOTHER

DAY 8: GOD'S BELOVED DAUGHTER AND PRECIOUS SPOUSE

Yesterday, at the conclusion of our first week of preparation, we saw how Mary reveals to us in a beautiful way the three "primary" relationships for which God has created us: childhood, spousehood, and parenthood.

Just as in human life these three relationships exist in a dynamic union with one another, so the same is true on the spiritual and supernatural level. Each one of us is born as a child of our parents, and we start out in a state of complete dependency upon their love, their shelter, and their care. And to the degree that we welcome this love and this foundational relationship, we will mature into authentic love, acceptance, and reciprocal self-giving. And then there comes a point when our capacities for love blossom also in the readiness and the desire for the unique depth and reciprocity—and the particular union, indissolubility, and fruitfulness—of the spousal relationship. Finally, when this spousal union is lived authentically, as a true and complete mutual self-giving of the spouses, then the fruit of new life in parenthood springs forth spontaneously from this union.

We see, then, how childhood is the root and branch from which spousal love flowers; and the fruit of this flowering is the beauty of parenthood. In this way, too, these relationships come "full circle," for we began with childhood and we end with childhood again. The persons who were once little children themselves have now, through their love, cooperated in allowing God to bring forth a new child into the world. But not only this: the parents themselves are led back, anew, to experience the truth of their own childhood again, and more deeply still, through seeing it reflected in the face of their child. However, this is a childhood, not of the flesh, but of the spirit, in which the dispositions of radical trust and receptivity transcend one's human parents to find their home in the heavenly Father, who is consciously embraced at the Rock and Foundation of one's life, and whose Love is welcomed as cradling and sheltering one's entire existence.

In being the root and branch of our whole existence, therefore, childhood is in no way something that is "left behind" for the sake of the other relationships. Rather, it would be more accurate to say that it is the *all-enveloping mystery* in which the other relationships can authentically unfold. It is never for a single moment necessary to separate ourselves from this truth of childhood before God; rather, this is the very foundation of our life *at every moment*, within which spousal and parental love truly blossom and bear fruit.

We also see how *friendship* and *fraternity* themselves—these forms of relationship of which spousal love is simply a unique and intense expression—find their foundation in the reality of childhood. In other words, we can recognize ourselves as brothers and sisters—and grow in authentic friendship on the basis of mutual sharing—only because we are all children of a common Father, whose love has created us and binds us together.

Let us now try to see these three forms of relationship more deeply in the Virgin Mary. They can be discerned through contemplation of the scene of the Annunciation, when the angel Gabriel approaches Mary and speaks to her in the name of God. Here we can glimpse the fact that Mary is indeed enfolded in these three forms of relationship in an intense way: in *daughterhood*, in *spousehood*, and in *motherhood*.

> In the sixth month the angel Gabriel was sent from God to a city of Galilee named Nazareth, to a virgin betrothed to a man whose name was Joseph, of the house of David; and the virgin's name was Mary. And he came to her and said, "Hail, full of grace, the Lord is with you!" But she was greatly troubled at the saying, and considered in her mind what sort of greeting this might be. And the angel said to her, "Do not be afraid, Mary, for you have found favor with God. And behold, you will conceive in your womb and bear a son, and you shall call his name Jesus. He will be great, and will be called the Son of the Most High; and the Lord God will give to him the throne of his father David, and he will reign over the house of Jacob for ever; and of his kingdom there will be no end." And Mary said to the angel, "How shall this be, since I have no husband?" And the angel said to her, "The Holy Spirit will come upon you, and the power of the Most High will overshadow you; therefore the child to be born will be called holy, the Son of God. And behold, your kinswoman Elizabeth in her

old age has also conceived a son; and this is the sixth month with her who was called barren. For with God nothing will be impossible." And Mary said, "Behold, I am the handmaid of the Lord; let it be to me according to your word." And the angel departed from her. (Luke 1:26-38)

First of all, Mary is, and knows herself to be, a beloved *child* of the heavenly Father. When the angel Gabriel addresses her in greeting, it is this truth, above all, which he emphasizes. It is interesting that he does not call her by her natural earthly name—Mary—but rather gives her a new name, the name known only to God: *Kekaritomene*. This Greek word, usually translated as "full of grace," is very rich in meaning. The root word *charis* means gift, grace, favor, or love bestowed from one to another. And the form of the word is a passive perfect participle, meaning that it is past, present, and future all at once—indicating an enduring, constant, and unbroken state, and one that is received from another (passively). Therefore, we can understand Mary's own unique name as meaning: **you who have been, are, and ever will be loved by God**.

This pure and abiding gift of God's love for Mary is the source of her authentic and unrepeatable personal identity. It is, in other words, precisely God's love which makes her the person who she is. This "belovedness" is indeed the truth of *childhood,* in which she unceasingly dwells. Mary is, in her deepest truth, *God's beloved daughter.* This is the all-enveloping truth in which the rest of her life unfolds, the root from which all things spring and from which they never depart.

Indeed, it is precisely Mary's joyful awareness of her belovedness before God that enables her to open her heart and her life to welcome God as he comes to her. She can open herself as a *bride* precisely because she is aware of God's intense love for her; she can receive his gift of self because she already knows his utter trustworthiness, his utter desire for her good, and his utter beauty—revealed through the Love that has gently cradled her from her earliest days. This gift of childhood, therefore, blossoms in Mary's heart into a total and radical *bridal receptivity to God.* She receives, as it were, God's "marriage proposal," which comes to her through the message of the angel. And she responds with her whole being: "Let it be to me according to your word" (Luke 1:38).

This act of complete consent by Mary is a "seal" set upon the gift of God's Love, which Mary has received from the first instant of her existence. It is, as it were, a "consecration" or complete entrustment in love, through which she places her entire life in God's hands. And her consent to God's Love is itself dependent upon this prior gift of his Love. In other words, when God offers an invitation of love to her, the invitation itself contains the grace of her response.

When Mary consents to this Love, she is freely affirming and making her own the gift that always precedes, accompanies, and sustains her. Her loving assent is, in a word, her "binding of self" to the Beloved, in a total and irrevocable way. And yet this "binding" is itself but an expression that she has already been bound by the gentle embrace of God's all-enfolding Love. She is simply saying yes to the reality of Love that already holds her, and thus allowing this Love to irradiate and transform her life totally and unreservedly:

> I am yours forever, and I want nothing, absolutely nothing, to separate me from you. I give myself into your hands totally, in trust and simplicity, and aflame with the longing of love. And in this surrender I give you complete permission to take possession of my life, of all that I am, within the mystery of your Love. You do not even need to ask me again, in the future, whether I will say "yes" to what you desire. You do not need to confer with me, my Love, about whether I am willing. I give you, in this moment, my willingness and my "yes" forever. Simply do anything and everything that you desire, for me, in me, and through me…for I know that it is all Love and only Love.

Reflection Questions:

— Do I find myself living habitually from this place of "belovedness" which is the deepest truth of who I am?

— Or do I live from another place? If so, what is this place from which I habitually think, live, and act? Can I open myself to welcome God's Love, allowing him to draw me into the shelter of his embrace—or rather to reveal to me that I am always cradled in his Love at every moment?

— Do I see in my heart the desire to give myself totally to God, to "bind" myself to him through total and unconditional surrender—in other words, to be intimately united to him in spousal love?

DAY 9: VIRGIN BRIDE AND FRUITFUL MOTHER

Let us continue speaking about these three relationships—childhood, spousehood, and parenthood—that we discern in the person of Mary. We spoke about her deepest identity before God as that of a *beloved child*, the truth of her belovedness, which is revealed in the gift of her "divine name": *kekaritomene*, or *she who has been, is, and ever will be loved by God*. Then we saw how her awareness of this awesome love of God—the conviction of God's total, everlasting, and unconditional love for her, which is the source of her own unique personal beauty—opens her heart to a "bridal" receptivity to God's invitation and his desire to give himself to her.

This bridal consent of Mary, since it springs from the perfect love of God for her, is total, pure, and irrevocable. This is because her assent is without the least shadow of sin, which, as we have seen, is precisely the "wound" of fear which causes us to turn away from the cradling arms of Love, grasping instead for a false independence. This fear is rooted, further, in a loss of trust in the absolute goodness of our heavenly Father, such that we lose the confidence, simplicity, and freedom of childhood before him. We begin to fear that his love for us is unreal or inauthentic—that he wants to "lord" his power over us, or wants to "use" and "dispose" of us as a mere instrument for his divine purposes. But our hearts spontaneously recoil from such a vision of God, because deep inside we thirst to be loved absolutely and for our own sake. We thirst, in other words, to be completely known and loved as we are, to be cradled within the sheltering love of another…and in this love to be intimately desired, with no other reason than that the other is drawn to us in love and in the desire to hold us in their embrace.

This deep thirst for love within us, this thirst to be known, loved, and desired, and to be united to the beloved within this love…this is not a lie. God himself has impressed this desire upon our heart, and it reveals, more than anything else, his own desire for us. Our thirst is simply an expression of his deeper thirst for us. It is the "imprint" of his loving gift sealed forever on our inmost being—this "virgin-point" that we spoke of previously. To get back in touch with this inmost truth of who we are before him…this is to get back in touch with the mystery of belovedness before God: with the truth of being his beloved child and precious spouse.

Therefore, what we see so clearly in Mary—her awareness of God's love, and of being a child and spouse—is completely true for each one of us as well. Mary knows that God is the most tender Father, the most loving Spouse, whose will is identical with his love, and whose ardent thirst is simply to unite his children intimately to himself, now and for all eternity. This awareness of the *total* love of God, therefore, awakens and sustains her own *total* response of love.

Thus, when Mary hands herself over into God's hands, it is completely and forever. Nonetheless, this handing-over is made present and alive—it becomes "incarnate"—in each succeeding moment of her life. Though she has given herself totally to God and has given him complete permission to touch her and to act in her life, God does not simply "use" her without eliciting anew at every moment her free and conscious "yes." And indeed his intention is not to "use" her at all, but to love, embrace, and cherish her for her own sake. Only from this space of absolute cherishing, absolute intimacy sought for its own sake, does the movement of "cooperation" flow. In other words, from the reality of *intimacy*, which is God's absolute desire for each one of us, the reality of *creativity and fruitfulness* also blossoms, in which we share in the outpouring of his love in this world.

God utterly respects and reverences Mary at every moment of her life, and never does anything in her or through her without seeking her willingness, her loving and trust-filled acceptance. The Annunciation is the first and most vivid expression of this profound respect of God, bending down to ask the permission of his creature to pour out into her and through her the immensity of his love. This is above all simply because **her "yes" is actually what he desires more than anything else— that is, the free love of her heart willingly given, so that he may unite her intimately to himself**. Anything else just flows from this fundamental "yes" of love, in which the heart of Mary is joined to the heart of God in intimate love—in which the two "Yeses," that of God and that of Mary, encounter and interlace in a profound unity. They are like two rings that have been interlocked and, while remaining distinct, are inseparably joined to one another.

From this union of "Yeses"—and even more, from this union of hearts—all fruitfulness and goodness spring forth. In Mary's case, this is first of all the very supreme "fruit of her womb," the incarnate Son of God, Jesus Christ, whom she consents to conceive precisely in her bridal "yes" to God. And later in her life, God seeks her "yes" again in a profound way by asking for her loving and compassionate presence at the foot of the Cross of Jesus. Here her openness to God flowers in the fruitfulness that makes her the Mother of all the faithful—of all those who are born from the complete gift of Christ's love on the Cross, begotten from the blood and water that flow from his pierced Heart.

Mary stands here at the foot of the Cross in faith—in complete trust in the goodness and love of God, which gently cradles her and her Son even in the darkest place. And here her "yes" matures and expands in a profound way, such that she is truly the Bride receiving the gift of the heavenly Bridegroom, Jesus Crucified, and giving herself to him in return. From the side of Christ—and through Mary's loving presence to receive this gift—all of the children of God are conceived and born throughout history. **In Mary's virginal receptivity at the foot of the Cross, her life is like a "womb" to receive the life-giving gift of Jesus, and to bear it for the sake of the entire world.** Therefore she stands, forever, at the very heart of the Church, from which, as from a wellspring, all the activities and movements of grace and salvation in this world flow, and to which they return.

Reflection Questions:

— *What stood out to me the most from this reflection? Why might this be the case?*

— *Do I see how Mary's abiding always at the "virgin-point" of her inmost heart in belovedness before God also allowed her to abide at the foot of the Cross, receiving in virginal love the gift of Jesus Crucified?*

— *There is a direct connection between receptivity to God and authentic love for others. To the degree that my heart is open to accept God's love for me, I can also accept others and cherish them with the same love I have first received. How can I deepen my living of this truth?*

DAY 10: PRAYER – PROXIMITY TO THE HEARTH OF HEALING LOVE

In the previous reflection, we saw how Mary, in her loving and trust-filled bridal receptivity, became the Mother, not only of Jesus, but of all the children of God. And we emphasized that her receptivity was only possible because she knew herself to be unceasingly and totally cradled within God's all-enveloping Love. Because of the security that such an awareness gave her, she was able to yield herself up to the touch of grace, to abandon herself in childlike confidence into the hands of her loving Father. In this way she shared in the innermost disposition of Jesus himself, who lived at every moment as the beloved Son of the Father, in and from that deep mystery of who he is as the Father's eternal Son.

Mary and Jesus, living as God's beloved within this world, have opened up a space which each one of us is invited to inhabit. Just as Adam and Eve, before original sin, dwelt in "belovedness," in complete childlike openness before God and one another, so Jesus and Mary— the New Adam and the New Eve—live this attitude once again, and thus restore it to our world. They have shown us the beauty of authentic childhood—this profound trust in the love of God, which awakens in us the desire and ability to entrust our lives entirely into his hands. They speak to us unceasingly, their voices echoing in prayer, echoing throughout our life, echoing through our Mother the Church:

> *Come… Come, little one, into the sanctuary of your heart, where we await you. Come to let yourself be loved by the God who knows you, delights in you, and desires to unite you intimately to himself. You are thirsty…and God wants to satisfy this thirst with his own closeness, with his own enveloping embrace. Only pronounce your "yes" and we will fill you with the torrent of Love.*

> *And if you find yourself afraid to say "yes," then simply do not flee…simply remain in this place and let yourself be gazed upon, let yourself be known, and let yourself be held. You will experience this Love holding you and infusing your life secretly with grace. Then this Love will itself beget in you the*

"yes" that you are afraid to pronounce. God's absolute "Yes" of love for you —his total affirmation of your unique beauty in his eyes—will awaken your "yes" in return, your acceptance of this awesome gift.

In order to help us enter more deeply into this inner sanctuary, to open ourselves to God's loving gaze, in this reflection we will begin to speak about prayer. What is prayer? We have, really, been speaking about it all along. It is, ultimately, simply a matter of letting oneself be know and loved by God (which we always are!). It is thus **getting in touch with the innermost truth of who we are, and with the Love that sustains us and the whole universe at every moment.** Simply to sit in his gaze of love, simply to rest within his enveloping Love...this is the heart of prayer.

Everything else that occurs in prayer occurs within this primary and all-enveloping rest within the knowledge and love of God. Even our own reciprocal gaze, in which we look upon the One who looks upon us, is itself contained within God's primary and inviting gaze. Even our thirst to rest against God's loving Heart is but a response to the fact that his Heart is already close to us, touching us and holding us.

There is a profound truth here that we have seen in our previous reflections, which should be made more explicit now: **we can only see ourselves in the light cast from the eyes of another.** Indeed, we are always, in a way, seeing ourselves through the eyes of others. Therefore, we are tempted to try to make ourselves "presentable" and "lovable" before them, even if this means projecting a false image of who we are. This is how deeply our own identity is tied up with the gaze of others. But this often ends up being an "exile" from our authentic inner truth, rather than is discovery. We need, instead, to encounter the gaze of love that goes deeper, that pierces through the brokenness, the fears, the false projections, and touches, knows, and loves us in the innermost reality of who we are.

Ultimately, we know this, we know that we are deeper than what others see. Therefore, our deepest understanding of ourselves corresponds with what we think that *God* sees when he looks upon us. The problem is that often this image does not correspond with what God truly sees, but rather with our own wounds and fears, our own projections of who he is and of who we are before him. Prayer, in this perspective, is simply a matter of **allowing ourselves to be bathed in the**

light cast from his loving eyes. In this way we enter into the deepest and most authentic truth of who we are before him. We can find ourselves liberated from the false and uncomprehending vision of others, who do not truly see us as we are, and even from our own narrow and limited vision...in order to allow God to show us how he sees us, and thus to give us the ability to see with his own vision.

From this place in which we allow ourselves to be beheld by God, deeply known and loved by him, **a profound intimacy grows and blossoms**. Prayer is therefore sitting at Christ's feet, like Mary of Bethany, receiving the love that flows unceasingly from him. Or indeed it is leaning against his bosom, as the beloved disciple, receiving the tender and loving reverberations of his Sacred Heart. It is a matter of letting ourselves be drawn to this burning Hearth of Love, emitting light and warmth in the darkness and chill of this world. Here we allow his radiance to bathe us in its splendor, and the heat of his Love to thaw the rigidity of our fear and our pain, until we become soft in his warmth, relaxed and surrendered in childlike trust.

Through this profound intimacy with Jesus, whose Heart is the burning Hearth of Love in which the whole Trinity dwells, we are taken up into the Son's own relationship with his Father, into the dynamic flow of love that is ever occurring between the Father, Son, and Holy Spirit. This is our highest calling and our breathtaking destiny: to be immersed into the innermost life of the Blessed Trinity, caught up into the very relationships of love that unite the Father, Son, and Holy Spirit to one another for all eternity! We are caught up into the space between the Father and the Son, in which they forever whisper, in the Breath of the Spirit, to one another, and to each of us: *I love you... I love you... I love you...*

We live in a world, however, that places so much emphasis on "doing" and "achieving"—even making these the source of our identity—that we can find this kind of restfulness and receptivity very difficult. So many do not know their identity as a beloved child of the Father, and therefore seek it in a thousand other places...when it is right here always in the depths of the heart, in that place where the Father is unceasingly looking upon us and loving us. This is what God desires so much to reveal to us again: to reveal to us his Love, and that his most ardent desire is simply that we rest in his arms, in the place of belovedness where nothing matters but the intimacy of union for which he created us.

This all-enfolding Love of God is present and at work in every moment and circumstance of our lives, even when we do not see it or feel it. Because we have lost our awareness of this Love, because we have lost the fullness of living relationship with the One who enfolds us in himself, Jesus came among us as one of us, touching us in our most painful, most wounded, and darkest places. The light of his loving gaze pierces the depths of our darkness, our pain, our shame. In this way he has reopened these places, these experiences to the radiant light of Love, to its consoling and healing warmth. Prayer is simply a matter of letting ourselves be drawn into proximity to this healing Fire…or rather, a matter of opening our souls to the touch of this Fire that already gently encompasses us, to this light of God's gaze which completely knows us, and in completely knowing us completely loves us.

Reflection Questions:

— *Do I see how Jesus and Mary have lived the attitude of childlike trust and surrender that Adam and Eve lost in the beginning? Do I believe that I, too, am capable of living this, through their gift and the support of divine grace?*

— *What is my experience of prayer? Do I feel like I am able to open myself to God's healing gaze and to the sheltering and consoling Fire of his Love?*

— *If I struggle with this, how could I let myself be drawn deeper into an encounter with God's Love? Do I need to devote more time to prayer? Do I need to turn to him more habitually in times of trail? Do I need to "look deeper" to the depths of my authentic desires and fears, so that I can experience his gaze in these places?*

DAY 11: AUTHENTIC FRUITFULNESS – CONTEMPLATIVE RECEPTIVITY

The whole Paschal Mystery of Jesus' Passion and Resurrection is ultimately about re-opening our closed and fearful hearts to the Love of God that ever envelops us within itself. Jesus penetrates into our loneliness and isolation in order to reopen it from the inside to the expansiveness of God's own embrace. In this way he immerses us again into that "torrent of love" that ever passes between himself and his Father, so that we may share, like our Virgin Mother, in the intimacy of the Trinity itself.

When we consent to receive this awesome gift of Love, to let ourselves be drawn near to the burning Hearth of God's immense Tenderness, then we find ourselves gradually healed and transformed by the divine touch. We are reconciled with our authentic personal truth in the eyes of God and allow him to unite us, through his pure grace, to himself. In this way we become, like Mary, daughter, spouse, and mother (or son, spouse, and father), by experiencing the joy of *adoption* and of resting in the Father's love, of *nuptial union* with Jesus who gives himself to us and welcomes us into himself, and of *fruitfulness* through the overshadowing and impregnating power of the Spirit of Love.

As we have seen, these three are like concentric circles, each contained within the other: *childhood* enfolding all the rest, and *spousal union* blossoming within childhood, and this union itself bearing abundant fruit in a sacred *paternity and maternity*. All childhood, spousehood, and parenthood in this world participate in these realities as they exist, in their most eminent and perfect form, in the life of the Father, Son, and Holy Spirit. In other words, the Source and Archetype of all childhood and nuptiality exists in the eternal union between the Father and the Son in their one Spirit, in the ardent flame of Love that passes ceaselessly between them, and in their mutual acceptance and surrender of self. And God's eternal creativity, even before the creation of the world, is that "from which all fatherhood on heaven and earth takes its name" (Eph 3:15): that mystery by which the Father eternally begets his beloved Son within the "womb" of the enfolding Spirit, and that mystery of the Spirit's procession from the shared union of the Father and the Son, which is overflowingly fruitful.

We were created to share in this Mystery of the Trinitarian Intimacy…the blessed communion of the Father, Son, and Holy Spirit. This is not only the deepest and most foundational *origin* of our life and our dignity, but also our central and highest *vocation and destiny*. And in our human relationships we already image and reflect this Mystery, in an imperfect but real way. Nonetheless, childhood, spousehood, and parenthood in this world are only images, and point beyond themselves to the fullness of Reality in which alone our hearts can be at rest. It is in our relationship and union with *God himself* that we pass fully from image to Reality, from reflection to the fullness of Light: into the truth of childhood before our true and heavenly Father, into the indwelling love of spousal union with the Bridegroom Jesus, and into that beautiful "spilling over" of love and creativity that blossoms from this union in the eternal fecundity of the Holy Spirit.

Let us talk more deeply, now, about the true meaning of fruitfulness —and therefore of maternity and paternity, indeed of all creativity in word and act within this world. **All true and enduring fruitfulness, in order to truly make God present in the fullness of his Mystery, must spring from a prior and abiding contemplative receptivity, such that we conceive his grace and life within us by the power of the Holy Spirit, and therefore allow him to make himself more deeply present in our world.**

This is the meaning, for example, of Jesus' parable on the seed that is scattered on the ground, with only certain kinds of soil allowing the seed to sprout, grow, and bear fruit:

> A sower went out to sow. And as he sowed, some seeds fell along the path, and the birds came and devoured them. Other seeds fell on rocky ground, where they had not much soil, and immediately they sprang up, since they had no depth of soil, but when the sun rose they were scorched; and since they had no root they withered away. Other seeds fell upon thorns, and the thorns grew up and choked them. Other seeds fell on good soil and brought forth grain, some a hundredfold, some sixty, some thirty. (Matthew 13:3-8)

It is profoundly important to realize that *the seed bears fruit of its own power*, if only the soil yields itself up entirely to it and nourishes, shelters, and protects it. This is central to what prayer and contemplation is all about. It is about becoming good soil in which the seed of the Word can implant itself and bear abundant fruit. Here, again, the Virgin Mary is the most perfect example: for it was she, before anyone else, who offered her entire being in contemplative and virginal receptivity to the seed of the Word, conceiving him literally within her heart and in her womb.

But this contemplative receptivity, as we have seen, did not end with the Annunciation, nor after the nine months of pregnancy were concluded. Rather, this receptivity was Mary's most central and enduring attitude throughout her entire life. Saint Luke, who most probably spoke with her directly and in depth about her experience (for how else could he know about the events of the first two chapters of his Gospel?), makes a point of this contemplative receptivity. He portrays her very explicitly as the one who is "good soil" for the Word—the Word who is Jesus Christ himself. Her first assent to God's invitation is her "Let it be to me according to your word" at the Annunciation (Lk 1:38), but then this assent is renewed and perpetuated at every moment of her life afterwards. When the shepherds come to see the Christ Child and the choir of angels cries out in the heavens, Luke says that "Mary kept all these things, pondering them in her heart;" and again, after the finding of the twelve year old Jesus in the temple after three days: "his mother kept all these things in her heart" (Lk 2:19; 2:51).

Mary has conceived already through faith and brought Christ physically into the world, but her abiding love and acceptance also allows her to lay her being open for the ever-deeper revelation of the mystery of God and his Love. In this way her journey is not ended with the birth of Christ, but continues to progress ever more deeply into the immensity of God's Love, and also dilates ever more universally to encompass his desire for the salvation of all. God, for his part, can do immense and beautiful things in and through her, precisely because her heart is a pure dwelling-place for the gift of his Love and surrenders to this Love unconditionally.

In her he finds the home that he seeks, the space in which he can pour out the torrent of generosity which overflows from his Heart. Further, her contemplative surrender allows God to draw her into the awesome mysteries of the life of Christ as they unfold before her eyes. Indeed, her surrender allows God to draw her into the most intimate depths of his own Trinitarian Being. Is it not she who abides, full of faith, at the foot of the Cross of Jesus, when the faith of the others falters? We already saw that she is there to receive the outpouring gift of the divine Bridegroom's love as it flows from his opened Heart. And she bears this gift within her without ceasing, conceiving again as the "archetype" or "model" of the Church, in order to bring forth perpetually from the fount of Baptism new children of the heavenly Father.

We see this mystery of conception and birth symbolized so beautifully in the liturgy of the Easter Vigil. After the commemoration of the mystery of Christ's passage through the darkness of this world as the burning Flame that brings light to fallen humanity, and after the inbreaking joy of his Resurrection, the celebration of Baptism begins. Those who have been preparing, through the period of the catechumenate, now come forward for their rebirth into the fullness of life as children of God, their sharing in the most precious fruit of the Paschal Mystery of Christ. Before the sacrament of Baptism is administered, however, the new water of the font is blessed. But how is it blessed? It is not blessed as on other days, with a simple prayer and gesture of the sign of the cross. Rather, it is blessed and sanctified—made life-bearing and fruitful—*by the descent of the Easter Candle, the symbol of Christ, into it three times.* This symbolizes the mystery of the Bridegroom's outpouring love entering into the receptive womb of the bridal Church, in order to make her fruitful as the Mother of all the faithful.

Now this awesome mystery is true not only of the universal Church, nor even of Mary, the most eminent member of this Church, *but of every individual soul.* We are all invited to be "mothers" of Christ by welcoming his gift and conceiving through his divine power at work within us. Indeed, we can say that authentic fatherhood itself must be immersed in this bridal and maternal mystery, so as itself to become transparent to the authentic light and love of God himself. Whether man or woman, our primary and all-encompassing attitude is meant to be, like the Virgin Mary, one of loving and trust-filled contemplative receptivity to the love and the gift of God.

Reflection Questions:

— *Do I see my deepest vocation—the fulfillment of my desires—as sharing in the intimacy of the Father, Son, and Holy Spirit? If not, in what do I place my hope instead?*

— *Do I find in myself tendencies to the "activism" that is so prevalent in our culture? Do I place "doing" over "being"? Or "productivity" over the authentic fruitfulness that springs from contemplative receptivity?*

DAY 12: A HOME FOR THE TRINITY

In the previous reflection we spoke about the innermost mystery of authentic fruitfulness as contemplative receptivity to the gift of God. Mary is the most radiant icon of this radical receptivity and of the abundant fruit that it allows to blossom. In her trust-filled "yes" to God's love and his invitation, she binds together all the hopes, desires, and aspirations of history, all of the longings and prayers of the Old Covenant. In this respect, she is truly "Daughter Zion," the woman who sums up in her personal existence the whole existence of her people, and opens its completely to God. The prophecy of Zephaniah is thus fulfilled in her:

> Sing aloud, O daughter Zion; shout, O Israel!
> Rejoice and exult with all your heart,
> O Daughter of Jerusalem!
> On that day it shall be said to Jerusalem:
> "Do not fear, O Zion;
> let not your hands grow weak.
> The LORD, your God, is in your womb,
> a warrior who gives victory;
> he will rejoice over you with gladness,
> he will renew you in his love." (Zeph 3:14, 16-17)

Mary, in her childlike and virginal openness to God, is truly one of the "little ones" of the Almighty, who are blessed by him in their poverty, because their hearts depend upon him alone in total faith. In this way she is able to welcome the very Incarnation of the Son of God in her womb, as is so beautifully (and surprisingly!) prophesied in the words of Zephaniah, as well as in the famous words of Isaiah: "Behold, a virgin shall conceive and bear a son, and shall call his name Emmanuel," which means God-is-with-us (Is 7:14). Mary's consent allows the divine Wellspring to inhabit her very body, and to unleash itself in and through her so as to irrigate the entire world with its presence.

When we open ourselves to this "Marian" receptivity, we allow our own heart and life to become "good soil" for the seed of the Word, which is ultimately Jesus Christ himself, who comes to us and pours his love into our hearts. Further, through his coming to us by the power of the Holy Spirit, Jesus brings with him the full mystery of the Father. Therefore our contemplative openness to welcome this gift allows the entire Trinity to take up his abode within our hearts. Our being becomes, in a real and profound way, a "home" for the Most Holy Trinity, as Jesus himself said during the Last Supper: "If a man loves me he will keep my word, and my Father will love him, and we will come to him and make our home with him" (John 14:23).

The reality of "home" and the reality of "keeping the word" are deeply connected. The word *to keep* in this case means much more than mere obedience to an external commandment; rather, it also implies *guarding, watching over*, or *sheltering*. This is exactly what we saw in the previous reflection on being good soil, or even a womb, for the word and the love of God. When we open our hearts in order to welcome Christ's word, whenever we make our being a shelter for his gift and his will, then he can come, with the Father and the Holy Spirit, and inhabit us in the most profound and intimate way.

But indeed our very ability to open ourselves in this way is itself God's gift, as his grace precedes, awakens, and sustains our own loving response. This is, in particular, the unique work of the Holy Spirit, who dwells within us and prays in us, teaching us how to pray by incorporating us into his own prayer. As Saint Paul wrote:

> The Spirit helps us in our weakness; for we do not know how to pray as we ought, but the Spirit himself intercedes for us with sighs to deep for words. And he who searches the hearts of men knows what is the mind of the Spirit, because the Spirit intercedes for the saints according to the will of God. (Romans 8:26-27)

The Spirit's presence and grace alive in our hearts cradles and sustains our own response, so that our every prayer, our every encounter with God, is a matter of "grace encountering grace." In other words, the *grace-within-us* through the indwelling of the Holy Spirit makes us able to receive the *grace-outside-of-us*, which comes through the gift of God incarnate in Christ, and made present in all the circumstances of our life in which he makes himself known.

We see in this intimate movement of prayer, therefore, a profoundly beautiful dynamic: the Spirit draws us to the Son and makes us able to welcome him, and the Son in turn draws us in himself to the Father and also allows us to welcome the Father. Within this "drawing," further, there is a twofold movement, two movements going in "opposite" directions which are actually the same: 1) we pass in the Spirit through the Son to the Father, so that we may abide in his bosom, 2) and we welcome the Father in the Son through the Spirit into the recesses of our own hearts, so they may make their home within us. This is the most breathtaking intimacy, which God ardently desires to have with each one of us. "May they all be one, Father; even as you are in me, and I in you, may they also be in us" (cf. John 17:21).

We are invited to share in the mutual indwelling of the three divine Persons, who each "inhabit" one another in the most blissful intimacy of love. If we are willing to give our "yes," then the Father, Son, and Holy Spirit come to make their home in us, dwelling in our hearts and breathing forth in us the fragrance of their love and joy. And by doing this, they are simultaneously enfolding us in their own most intimate embrace, such that we find our home in them, in the eternal communion that they share.

This, indeed, is not only the greatest gift we can possibly receive—the reality that encompasses all of life and gives it meaning—but it is also the greatest gift we can offer to our brothers and sisters. If we truly allow the Trinity to live within us, giving him a place of welcome and repose in our inmost heart and life, then the fragrance of his Love will necessarily spread through us to others. Indeed, the Trinity brings with him the ceaseless hymn of his own life of perfect love and joy, and the echoes of this sacred music, this song of jubilation, through sounding in our hearts, will be heard by others, attracting them to God.

In welcoming the indwelling presence of God, indeed, we find that he is able to perpetuate within us his saving mysteries, his redeeming and healing activity in the world. Christ comes to live so deeply within us that he perpetuates in us his own life and the mysteries of his existence: his Incarnation, his prayer, his ministry, his compassion for humanity, his Transfiguration, his Passion, his Resurrection, his Ascension, and his gift of the Spirit. As the *Catechism of the Catholic Church* says:

> Christ enables us *to live in him* all that he himself lived, and *he lives it in us*. "By his Incarnation, he, the Son of God, has in a certain way united himself with each man" (*Gaudium et Spes,* 22.2). We are

called only to become one with him, for he enables us as the members of his Body to share in what he lived for us in his flesh as our model: "We must continue to accomplish in ourselves the stages of Jesus' life and his mysteries and often to beg him to perfect and realize them in us and in his whole Church. ... For it is the plan of the Son of God to make us and the whole Church partake in his mysteries and to extend them to and continue them in us and in his whole Church. This is his plan for fulfilling his mysteries in us" (St. John Eudes). (par 521)

Saint Elizabeth of the Trinity understood this so well when, in her *Prayer to the Trinity*, she wrote:

O my God, Trinity whom I adore, let me entirely forget myself that I may abide in You, still and peaceful as if my soul were already in eternity; let nothing disturb my peace nor separate me from You, O my unchanging God, but that each moment may take me further into the depths of Your mystery! Pacify my soul! Make it Your heaven, Your beloved home and place of Your repose; let me never leave You there alone, but may I be ever attentive, ever alert in my faith, ever adoring and all given up to Your creative action.

O my beloved Christ, crucified for love, would that I might be for You a spouse of Your heart! I would anoint You with glory, I would love You – even unto death! Yet I sense my frailty and ask You to adorn me with Yourself; identify my soul with all the movements of Your soul, submerge me, overwhelm me, substitute Yourself in me that my life may become but a reflection of Your life. Come into me as Adorer, Redeemer and Saviour.

O Eternal Word, Word of my God, would that I might spend my life listening to You, would that I might be fully receptive to learn all from You; in all darkness, all loneliness, all weakness, may I ever keep my eyes fixed on You and abide under Your great light; O my Beloved Star, fascinate me so that I may never be able to leave Your radiance.

O Consuming Fire, Spirit of Love, descend into my soul and make all in me as an incarnation of the Word, that I may be to Him a super-added humanity wherein He renews His mystery; and You O Father, bestow Yourself and bend down to Your little creature, seeing in her only Your beloved Son in whom You are well pleased.

O my "Three", my All, my Beatitude, infinite Solitude, Immensity in whom I lose myself, I give myself to You as a prey to be consumed; enclose Yourself in me that I may be absorbed in You so as to contemplate in Your light the abyss of Your Splendour!

We see in this prayer not only Elizabeth's profound desire for God, but her awareness of God's immense desire for her. She is, as it were, simply responding to an invitation, to the awareness that her beloved "Three" yearn to take up their abode within her, and in doing so to irradiate her whole being with their life, love, joy, and activity. So she offers herself happily and lovingly to the Trinity, welcoming him radically into her soul, knowing herself to be his beloved daughter and spouse. How beautifully, in this young woman of the early twentieth century, do we see reflected the attitude of that other young woman of the first century, when God first incarnated himself within our world!

Reflection Questions:

— *What is my spontaneous emotional and spiritual response to the affirmation that the entire Trinity desires to make his "home" within me?*

— *Do I understand how the greatest gift that I can offer to the world is precisely my receptivity to God and his gift?*

— *In thinking that Christ desires to "incarnate" himself in my life and to perpetuate in me his saving mysteries, what is my response? Do I desire this? Am I afraid of this?*

DAY 13: ABIDING AT THE SOURCE OF UNITY

In yesterday's reflection we spoke about how the Trinity desires to make his home in our hearts, to dwell within us in ineffable intimacy. We also said that this indwelling of God within us is also, simultaneously, his welcoming of us into the Home of his own innermost life of love. This mutual indwelling is the deepest desire of God and the culmination of the prayer and the saving work of Jesus himself, who prayed that "all may be one, Father; as you are in me and I am in you, may they also be in us." Further, in this mutual indwelling, God is able to perpetuate in us the mysteries of the life of Christ, allowing a kind of "extended incarnation" to occur within our hearts and lives, as God's Love reaches out in and through us to make itself present in every time and place.

In this reflection, there is a second element of this "indwelling" that we also want to speak about—a second element of the mystery of "home." We said that we are invited to open ourselves as a "home" for the Blessed Trinity, but **we are also invited to be a "home" for each one of our brothers and sisters in this world**. Indeed, the first reality—letting God make his home in us—allows the second one to blossom. As we welcome the love that God has for us and open our hearts to let him come and dwell in us, our whole being is dilated and expanded by his presence.

As he makes his home in us it is even more true that he is welcoming us into the Home of his own Heart. Therefore, having found our Home in the Trinity, we are able to open our own hearts and lives for all of the thirsting hearts within this world. We can welcome them, love them, and accompany them—seeing and accepting them in the light of the same love that we have first received from God. In this way our love can become a space in which they glimpse the immensity of God's own love, in which they can taste the shelter of his own enveloping embrace.

The "home" of our own heart becomes a safe dwelling-place for them in this world, in which they truly find another person before whom they can share themselves, certain that they are reverenced, accepted, and authentically loved. And ultimately this concrete and intimate human love opens the way directly for others to encounter God and his own openness the welcome and to shelter them. In a way, our heart becomes a kind of "antechamber" through which they pass into the House of the Father, into the intimacy of his most gentle embrace. And here we all find ourselves, together, sheltered in the perfect unity of the Father, Son, and Holy Spirit, made one with our loving God and one, through him and in him, with one another.

All of this reveals to us the profound mystery that burns like a fire at the heart of every individual life—this most intimate mystery that gives meaning to everything else. This mystery is precisely **our belovedness before God, and his ardent desire to unite us to himself in intimate love**. What does this mean, concretely? It means that the primary vocation of every human being is *prayer*. It is our vocation to an unspeakably deep communion with God that transcends all the limited expressions of human intimacy in this world, while eminently fulfilling them. This is the most perfect union of Parent and child, the most intimate mutual indwelling of Bridegroom and bride, and also the radiant fruitfulness of love that spontaneously flows from this union.

The *contemplative life*, therefore, lies at the heart of every person's existence, whatever its external contours may be. It is the most intimate and interior form that gives meaning to everything else and expresses itself in the particular richness and multiplicity of the different vocations and circumstances of daily life. In other words, we are all invited to repose within the enveloping embrace of the Father, Son, and Holy Spirit...already in this life, and perfectly forever in the next. This movement into the embrace of God is the inner trajectory of our whole existence, since God has created us for precisely this purpose. On the other hand, this mystery of contemplative intimacy is also the center from which all spreads, like the ripples cast from a pebble thrown into still water.

To live a life of deep prayer, therefore, is to place one's life entirely into the hands of our loving Father, to give him permission to show himself to truly be our loving Father. And he will show us! It is also to embrace the deep desire in our heart for union with the divine Bridegroom, with the ineffable divine Beauty that touches and draws our hearts so powerfully, and in which alone we will be at rest. It is to *place the Most Holy Trinity at the very center of one's existence*, such that all things orbit around the pursuit of ever-deepening intimacy with him and radical receptivity to his gift. This also implies recognizing and living the *primacy of interpersonal intimacy* over all external tasks or achievements. By doing this we embrace and witness to the highest vocation of the human person, the one in which all secondary vocations find their context: *the vocation to love and intimacy, first of all with God, and then, in him, with our brothers and sisters.*

In summary, through prayer we are invited to *return to the Source*, from which the whole of creation ceaselessly flows through an act of God's perfect love, and in this way reunite with the very Foundation of all being. Further, this union with God, our Source and Foundation, is not only a matter of an individual, isolated life, but rather bears, and in a way unifies, the whole creation by carrying it back into the welcoming embrace of the Trinity. It allows all things to return again to their Wellspring and to find their consummation in his enveloping Love.

We can imagine this movement, for example, with the image of a *prism*, through which light passes. Before it touches the prism, the light is undivided in its heat and radiance, bearing all colors as one within its unified intensity. However, after passing through the prism its light is divided in a multiplicity of different colors. To enter into the heart of prayer and contemplation is to return to the space in which the prism first meets the light, welcoming its undivided and undimmed radiance.

This image is imperfect, as the unified light of God already bears in itself the fullness of all multiplicity and the richness of all color even before encountering the prism of creation, but nonetheless it is very insightful. The whole of created reality flows forth from the single mystery of God's Love, each being reflecting this Love in its own unique way. The same is true for every individual human person, each of whom manifests God's Light in an unrepeatable way in his or her concrete existence. Nonetheless, at the inmost core of the being of each one of us, we bear the seal of Infinite Love, the impress of Eternity, the mystery of Fullness. And therefore we long not just for partiality, not just for multiplicity, but for Fullness, Totality, and Unity.

We yearn to return to the Source, where our being is united to the fullness of Being, and where our uniqueness is wed in intimate love to the uniqueness of every other being—a uniqueness that is not destroyed by returning into the Unity of God, but rather consummated in the most eminent way. This is what occurs in the depths of our surrender to the Holy Trinity. We immerse ourselves in the undivided light of his Love, and in doing so we rediscover all things in abundant fullness, bound together as one within the perfect unity of his own all-encompassing Mystery.

Reflection Questions:

— *So many hearts within this world are thirsting for love and acceptance, for a "home" in the welcoming heart of another. Do I feel in myself the desire to offer my heart to others in this way? How?*

— *If intimacy with God in prayer is truly the central vocation of every human being, the ultimate destiny of each one of us, am I seeking and living this reality?*

— *Do I understand the image of the prism? What is my response to the reality that this image represents?*

DAY 14: A HOME WITHIN HER "YES"

We have seen that the contemplative life of love and intimacy lies at the very heart of human existence, as the space from which all flows and to which it returns. It is that space of unity, within the undivided light of God, where the unique existence of each one of us is not merely a "fragment" of the Mystery of God, nor merely a "ray" of divine Light, but is rather open to God's utter Fullness and is surrendered to his Totality. In this way we can allow ourselves to be cradled within the Immensity of God's all-embracing Love, this Love that encompasses the entire universe in the simplicity and oneness of its embrace.

This life of intimacy lies at the very center of the Church as the wellspring of her life and the summit of her existence...since she is, in a way, nothing but the "redeemed creation" already united to God, anticipating the consummation that awaits us in the new creation. In Mary we see this Mystery shining most vividly and clearly, since she is the one who has first welcomed this undivided Light in its fullness, and abandoned herself totally into the enfolding Love of God. She reveals to us, in her own unique existence, the vocation and destiny of each one of us. Mary reveals that **the very essence of the Church is intimacy with the Trinity—the sharing of humanity in the inner life of the Father, Son, and Holy Spirit, and the communion among men and women that blossoms within the Trinity's embrace**. The "center-point" around which the entire life of the Church orbits, therefore, and from which it derives its meaning, is precisely the "Marian mystery" of contemplative intimacy with God—this mystery of childlike and bridal receptivity to God's gift of himself, and the complete reciprocal gift of oneself to him in return.

Mary is thus, as it were, the "Church-in-person"—before the Church has yet come to her full visible expression in the world through body of the Apostles and the community of all those who believe in Christ. Because of this, the Marian mystery interiorly informs all the other elements of the Church: the hierarchical ministry of Peter and the Apostles, the mission of laity and religious in the world, and the whole of the Church's task of evangelization. Everything flows from and returns to this Marian center, which, for its part, is simply centered in Christ and in the Father in whose bosom he always rests.

In theological language, there is a term for the way that Mary represents the entire Church: it is called "corporate personality." This does not mean that an individual is "anonymously" absorbed into a corporate body or a community and loses his or her individuality. Rather, it means the exact opposite. It refers to the mysterious way in which an individual person, through their loving openness of heart, can "sum up" in himself or herself the life of a whole community, carrying them in their own life and prayer.

They "represent" in their individual existence the existence a great number of people, and thus are able to unify them within their own heart, drawing them together through the movement of their surrender to God. Abraham, for example, bore within himself the fullness of the chosen people to come, who would spring from him and the promise he received from God: "'Look toward heaven, and number the stars, if you are able to number them... So shall your descendants be.' And he believed the LORD; and he reckoned it to him as righteousness" (Genesis 15:5-6). In this he is a model of faith for all generations; indeed, he is the father of all the faithful, since he placed his faith radically in God and welcomed in this way the blessing that God desired to pour out in and through him.

Moses, too, lived this mystery, as he interceded for the Israelites, bearing their sins, burdens, and hopes within his own heart before God in prayer and intercession. We can see the same thing in the Prophets, who bore the infidelities and aspirations of their people, and in some way helped to tie the knot of communion with God that sin has torn asunder.

But in Christ alone does this mystery reach its fulfillment. In him this "bearing" of others reaches its full expression in the mystery of "vicarious atonement." In other words, since he is both God and man, he is able, literally and truly, to take every individual person throughout history up into his own Sacred Heart, into his own humanity, and in this way to draw us back into the welcoming embrace of the Father. He makes us one with God—and with one another—within the sinews of his own reconciling Heart.

Mary also lives this mystery in an intense way. Through her union with Christ, who bears all humanity as one within his unifying Body, she too comes, in her own way, to "represent" all of humanity. In her own filial and virginal "Yes" to God, she takes up the struggles and hopes of every human heart and ties them together with the cord of her own perfect consent. This "Yes" to Love, pronounced perfectly by Mary, is important for each and every individual person throughout history. **Because she has pronounced her "Yes" in the name of all and for the sake of all, she has created the "space" in which the "Yes" of each one of us can find a home, in which it can be awakened and sustained.**

This is how Mary lives the central mystery of the Church, since she pronounces, in her personal "Yes," the "Yes" which will encompass and hold all believers throughout history. When we allow ourselves to be inserted into Mary's "Yes," we find ourselves able to stand, with her and in her, close to Jesus Christ. Indeed, we allow ourselves to be taken, through her, into the very welcoming Heart of Jesus, who enfolds us in his embrace as in the most perfect Home…a Home which is ultimately the enveloping embrace of the entire Trinity, Father, Son, and Holy Spirit.

Reflection Questions:

— *Do I find in myself the desire for the Totality of God's Love, the yearning to reach beyond what is "partial" and "incomplete" to the fullness of the Trinity's embrace?*

— *Do I see the Church as the space of intimate communion with the Trinity (and of unity among humanity), or do I see her as a mere institution or social structure?*

— *In speaking of Mary's "Yes" as the space in which my own "Yes" can be awakened and sustained, we come right to the heart of the meaning of Marian consecration. Is this something that I desire to do: to place my own life, my own desire to say "Yes," within the enfolding "Yes" of Mary?*

WEEK 3

THE GREATEST GIFT: COMMUNION

DAY 15: THE UNIQUE AND UNIVERSAL MOTHER

The previous two weeks have been rather intense in "introspection," in both our looking deep into our own hearts, as well as in our trying to "see within" the mystery of reality and the Gospel to its innermost heart. Hopefully this has allowed us to get more deeply in touch with the awesome Love of God which upholds us in our own inner heart and also cradles the whole universe gently and ceaselessly within itself.

We have seen how the Virgin Mary, in a unique way, reveals the face of this Love to us—just as the mother is the first to reveal love to her newborn child. In this, Mary plays a beautiful and indispensable role in our own lives, namely, that of *revealing the face of God's Tenderness through her own maternal tenderness.* Since God is the origin of both masculinity and femininity, it was fitting that, in addition to becoming incarnate as a man in Christ, he also fashioned an individual woman who, in a special way, would reflect the "maternal" characteristics of his own divine Heart. We think, for example, of the beautiful words of Isaiah:

"Rejoice with Jerusalem, and be glad for her, all you who love her; rejoice with her in joy, all you who mourn over her; that you may suck and be satisfied with her consoling breasts; that you may drink deeply with delight from the abundance of her glory." For thus says the LORD: "Behold, I will extend prosperity to her like a river, and the wealth of the nations like an overflowing stream; and you shall suck, you shall be carried upon her hip, and dandled upon her knees. As one whom his mother comforts, so I will comfort you; you shall be comforted in Jerusalem." (Isaiah 66:10-13)

In these verses, God reveals that *he* is the one who comforts us as a tender mother, nursing us through the abundant nourishment of love that he gives us through "Jerusalem." But what, or who, is Jerusalem? Jerusalem here is a symbol, first of all, of the Church. As we have said, she is "Mother Church," in whom we are reborn as children of God and through whose life of prayer, sacraments, communion, and love we are nourished and fostered as children growing up to eternal life. In this respect the Church is indeed a "womb" for us within this world. She is the space in which we are sheltered and nourished throughout the dangers and insecurities of this life, so that, like infants in a mother's womb, we may be ready to go through the final passage: *the birth into the endless joy and security of heaven, which is nothing but God's everlasting embrace.* This embrace is the embrace of father, mother, and spouse all in one—the fullness of the endless bliss of Father, Son, and Holy Spirit.

But Jerusalem also refers, in a particular way, to the Virgin Mary. We saw this in our last reflection when we spoke about "corporate personality" and how Mary sums up in herself all the promises made to her people, realizing individually in her own life the vocation of Israel. In her the chosen people are completely open to welcome "the dawn from on high that shines upon us" through the tender compassion of God (Luke 1:78). Therefore, in her the Old Covenant is consummated in the New Covenant, and Israel passes over into the Church—at last united to God in the fullness of intimacy and in a bond of covenant love that can never be severed.

We have been inserted into this new and eternal covenant through our Baptism, and we partake of its consummation every time we approach the Sacrament of the Eucharist. We find ourselves, in other words, cradled within the bonds of intimacy that God has wrought through his own Love—uniting us to himself and to all of our brothers and sisters within the bosom of his one Church.

Just as we did not enter this world alone, nor grow in human maturity alone—but rather in and through a loving community—the same is true in the supernatural sphere. No one becomes a Christian alone. Rather, when our hearts are opened to receive the gift of faith, we always received this gift mediated through the community of all those who belong to God—through the Body of Christ—and find ourselves welcomed into the enfolding arms of this Body. All grace that flows forth from the Heart of Christ passes through the Church which Jesus himself established, and, in drawing us back to his welcoming Heart, also draws us into the intimacy of the Church's own life. The *Catechism of the Catholic Church* expresses this as follows:

> "Believing" is an ecclesial act. The Church's faith precedes, engenders, supports, and nourishes our faith. The Church is the mother of all believers. "No one can have God as Father who does not

have the Church as Mother" (St. Cyprian). (par 181)

Pope Benedict XVI said in one of his last general audiences:

> This faith [that I profess in Baptism] is not the result of my own solitary reflection, it is not the product of my thought; it is the fruit of a relationship, a dialogue, in which there is a listener, a receiver, and a respondent; it is communication with Jesus that draws me out of the "I" enclosed in myself to open me to the love of God, the Father. It is like a rebirth in which I am united not only to Jesus, but also to all those who have walked and are walking on the same path; and this new birth that begins with Baptism continues for the rest of my life. I cannot build my personal faith in a private dialogue with Jesus, because faith is given to me by God through a community of believers that is the Church and projects me into the multitude of believers, into a kind of communion that is not only sociological but rooted in the eternal love of God, who is in himself the communion of the Father and of the Son and of the Holy Spirit, it is Trinitarian Love. Our faith is truly personal only if it is also communal: it can be my faith only if it dwells and moves within the "we" of the Church, only if it is our faith, the common faith of the one Church. (October 31, 2012)

Yes, the Church is truly both a "womb" for us and our true "home" within this world. Indeed it is she who carries us over the boundary of death into eternity, since she exists not only in this world, but in heaven. Actually, the fullness of her reality, while made present within this world, is seen in radiant fullness only in heaven, where she is one with God "as a Bride prepared for her Husband" (Revelation 21:2).

The Church is therefore not a mere institution, or even a "society" in the normal political or sociological sense, as Pope Benedict so beautifully said. Rather, **she is a *communion*: the reality of all those who have been made to share in the intimacy of the Father, Son, and Holy Spirit.** And Mary stands not only as the first member of this family, but in a way as the one who shelters all others within the hearth of her own maternal love. This is because, through her total acceptance of God's love and her utter surrender to him, she allows her heart to be expanded beyond limits to *universal proportions*. Now **she is truly able, in her unique individual personality, to enfold all of humanity within her**

own loving heart. When we experience the beautiful sense of "home" within the one, holy, catholic, and apostolic Church, therefore, we are truly experiencing the embrace of Mary, the unique and universal Mother.

Reflection Questions:

— *Do I recognize that I have not become a Christian alone, but have received this gift mediated through the Church, and as an experience of being "inserted" into the community of all those who believe? What does this mean for me practically?*

— *In my experience of the Church's motherhood, can I discern the embrace of Mary's motherhood? Indeed, can I discern the tender "mothering" of almighty God?*

DAY 16: UNIFYING ALL THE LINES OF CONTRADICTION

Yesterday we saw that, just as our natural human life is sheltered from its earliest days within the love of a mother, so the same is true in our spiritual life. Indeed, there is a direct correlation between these two forms of life—natural and spiritual—as we tried to grasp during the first week of reflections. Our fundamental experience of love as a child sets the stage for the rest of our life by giving us the context in which to situate every future experience. This context is that of love and intimacy, of experiencing one's own existence flowing as a gift from another and sheltered within the all-enfolding love of another. Such an awareness, in turn, awakens a spirit of gratitude and the desire to give oneself in return.

Therefore, just as we have a mother in the natural sphere, God has also given us a mother in the supernatural sphere. Indeed, if our experience of motherly love in the natural sphere is broken and obscured—through neglect, abuse, or absence—God desires to heal our hearts through offering us a heavenly mother. This mother, Mary and the Church, gives us the love that we thirst for, the love that we so desperately need—and in doing so reveals the "maternal" love of our heavenly Father himself.

But what is this mother like? This, in part, was the purpose of the second week: to "get a feel" for the beauty of Mary, our spiritual mother. We saw that she is, most deeply, *the one who is aware that she is cradled ceaselessly in the arms of perfect Love, and who within this Love surrenders herself totally.* We saw that she is (and knows herself to be) a beloved *child*, and through the confidence that this childlikeness awakens, she opens herself also to be a *spouse* of God, the divine Bridegroom; finally, through her filial and spousal relationship with God, she becomes transparent as a *mother* to the outpouring of his healing, consoling, and transforming light.

In this, Mary is the model for each one of us, who have also been created to experience, profoundly, these relationships of filial, spousal, and parental love. Indeed, we said that Mary is more than merely a model; she opens in herself the very "space" in which the life of each one of us can unfold in communion with God. This is because her "Yes," though profoundly personal and utterly intimate, is not a merely private consent, but bears in itself the "Yes" of all believers throughout history. Indeed, it opens the way for our own "Yes" to be pronounced, since through it she welcomes the overshadowing grace of the Holy Spirit and lets Christ himself become incarnate within the world. In a word, through the marriage of humanity and divinity that occurs within Mary's virginal womb, not only is the Son of God made a Son of man, but the universal Church herself dawns in her full mystery for the first time within our world.

Mary herself is, in an ineffable way, both an individual woman and the innermost mystery of the universal Church, Virgin Bride of Christ and Mother of all the faithful. This is something that cannot be adequately defined in concepts or explained in words. Rather, it is something that can only be gazed upon in contemplation and experienced in life. The French poet, Paul Claudel, had such an experience. When he was still young, and rebelling against his earlier Catholic faith, he had an encounter with the "unique twofold mother" who is both Mary and the Church:

> There was…the young man of twenty-five who once followed the Office in Notre Dame with a mind still crammed with objections and a heart full of repulsion. One Christmas Eve, during the singing of the Magnificat, the whole faith of the Church burst in upon him. From then onward he came again and again to the old cathedral to take his theology course—his teacher being "the Holy Virgin herself, patient and majestic". With his face "pressed against the grille of the choir" he watched the Church living, and through that sight, which leaves the minds of so many in an apathetic inertia, he understood all. For, as he explained, "when Paul spoke to me, and Augustine made things clear to me, and Gregory broke bread for me with antiphon and response, the eyes of Mary above me were there to explain it all to me." The "maternal and reassuring majesty" that enveloped him was at one and the same time that of Mary and that of the Church, and indissolubly so. All he had to do was to find his support in that unique twofold Mother, without any further making of distinctions; the Mother

"who brings together in silence in her heart and reunites in one single hearth all the lines of contradiction".[i]

It is touching to find in this quote the image of the "hearth," which we have spoken of in previous reflections. Mary is the child-become-spouse, and the spouse-become-mother, who "brings together in silence in her heart and reunites in one single hearth all the lines of contradiction." We think of how fragmented, how "scattered" our own lives are by so many things. And we yearn to get back to a place of unity and simplicity, where we can let go of our distractions, fears, and compulsions and rest in the arms of another. **This is what Mary offers to us as the "twofold mother" who, as the hearth of love, draws us close to her bosom and warms us with the fire of God's Love that burns ceaselessly within her.**

She invites us, in other words, into the "silence of love" where her heart ever beats, without the need for words or explanations, in a ceaseless hymn of praise for the Blessed Trinity. This is her eternal Magnificat, which sounds throughout all the currents of history since she uttered it that first time in the land of Palestine. Indeed, Mary's silent hymn of praise is but an echo, a response, to the perfect hymn of the Trinity's own life of love and intimacy: the song of delight and jubilation ever resounding in the communion of the Father, Son, and Holy Spirit.

To conclude this reflection, let us read the words of Mary's Magnificat, and join our hearts with this hymn of love ceaselessly sounding:

My soul magnifies the Lord,
and my spirit rejoices in God my Savior,
for he has regarded the low estate of his handmaiden.
For behold, henceforth all generations
  will call me blessed;
for he who is mighty has done great things for me,
and holy is his name.
And his mercy is on those who fear him
from generation to generation.
He has shown strength with his arm,
he has scattered the proud
  in the imagination of their hearts,
he has put down the mighty from their thrones,

and exalted those of low degree;
he has filled the hungry with good things,
and the rich he has sent empty away.
He has helped his servant Israel,
in remembrance of his mercy,
as he spoke to our fathers,
to Abraham and to his posterity for ever.
(Luke 1:46-55)

Reflection Questions:

— *Considering the little "review" given of the previous two weeks, what stands out to me the most so far?*

— *Has my experience of the love of father or mother, on a natural human level, been imperfect or even broken? How can taking Mary in a special way as my mother help to heal this wound, and even to heal my relationship with the heavenly Father?*

— *What theme strikes me most clearly from the words of Mary's Magnificat?*

DAY 17: MOTHER OF UNITY

Yesterday we quoted the beautiful words of Paul Claudel that Mary is the unique twofold mother "who brings together in silence in her heart and reunites in one single hearth all the lines of contradiction." These words give us access to one of the most beautiful titles of Mary: **she is the Mother of Unity.** This also allows us to understand how she is indeed in a mysterious way "Mother Church" herself, the innermost mystery of the Church who, as Vatican II said, is the "sacrament" or "sign and instrument both of a very closely knit union with God and of the unity of the whole human race" (*Lumen Gentium*, par. 1). Through her profound and intimate union with the Holy Spirit—and through him with the entire Trinity—she truly becomes a servant of unity, indeed, as we saw, the very "hearth" in which all is drawn together into intimate loving communion. In this, Mary incarnates in the most perfect way the activity of the Holy Spirit himself, which is *unity*. Just as the Spirit is the Bond or Kiss of intimacy between the Father and the Son—the very space or "womb" of the Son's begetting and union with the Father—so within creation his work is always to bring about unity: unity with God and unity among humanity. Mary, irradiated by the Spirit's presence and totally docile to his touch, shares in this work with her entire being.

Thus, as we will see more deeply in a future reflection, Mary, through her union with the Spirit, opens up in and through herself the mystery of the Church. These three mysteries—the Spirit, Mary, and the Church—are profoundly and inseparably united in God's work of salvation. The Church is the "space" of unity, with God and with all of our brothers and sisters. This is because she is, like Mary, the Virgin Mother who is made fruitful by the Holy Spirit, and, indeed, reflects the very "divine maternal womb," who is the Spirit in the inner life of the Trinity. The Church, therefore, like Mary and through Mary, is the place in which "all the lines of contradiction"—of division, of hatred, of misunderstanding, of estrangement—are overcome within the unity of a single faith, a common hope, and an undivided love.

This is Mary's deepest and most intimate desire: that all the children

of God be one, bound together in a single faith and in the fullness of the Church's life, which has been entrusted to her by God. In this, Mary is simply reflecting in her own maternal heart the deepest longings and aspirations of the Spirit, of her Son, Jesus Christ, and of the eternal Father himself. On the night that Jesus was arrested, after unveiling his Sacred Heart before his disciples and giving himself to them in the Holy Eucharist, he prayed to his Father in their presence. And this is what he prayed for:

> I pray...for all those who believe in me through their word, that they may all be one; even as you, Father, are in me, and I in you, that they also may be in us, so that the world may believe that you have sent me. The glory which you have given me I have given to them, that they may be one even as we are one, I in them and you in me, that they may become perfectly one, so that the world may know that you have sent me and have loved them even as you have loved me. Father, I desire that they also, whom you have given me, may be with me where I am, to behold my glory which you have given me in your love for me before the foundation of the world. (John 17:20-24)

This prayer is so rich, so beautiful, that it deserves prolonged and repeated pondering. Let us only note a few central realities, which show forth the longing that burns like an ardent fire in the Heart of our Redeemer and our divine Spouse.

1) Jesus prays that all who believe throughout history will be united, and thus his prayer is universal in breadth and depth, stretching out through all time and space. There is not a single person who is not called into this intimate unity, whom the communion of the divine life is not meant to encompass and hold within the unity of a single Body. 2) Further, this kind of unity he prays for is not merely an "agreement" or harmony on the human level, but a true oneness on the very model of the intimacy of the three divine Persons themselves, indeed, a sharing in the oneness of the Trinity. Thus Christ's prayer reaches out not only in breadth and depth, but also in height...into the very bosom of the Holy Trinity, the perfect unity of the Father, Son, and Holy Spirit. 3) This unity of all who believe is to be "perfect," so deep and intimate that our unity becomes a kind of "mutual indwelling," as Jesus says: "as you are in me and I am in you, that they also may be in us." And we can

say that this also enables our "being in one another" through the very power of divine Love within us and binding us together.

4) This kind of unity can only come as a *gift*, and not merely as the result of our own efforts; it is therefore a grace to be received with open hearts in prayer and radical receptivity: "The glory which you have *given* me I have *given* to them, that they may be one even as we are one." 5) This unity is necessary for the authentic witness and mission of the Church in the world, since any division among her members hinders her transparency in truly being the "sacrament" of unity for the whole of humanity. It is precisely our unity which reveals the depths of God's own Trinitarian unity, and which has a "magnetic" effect in drawing all human hearts to the "Home of Communion" which is the Church.

6) Our unity is not only a gift of grace, but is indeed the fruit and expression of our awareness of being intimately and intensely loved by God. When we know ourselves, uniquely, to be loved, then we can also see this love shining on the faces of our brothers and sisters. This is what is revealed by Jesus' words: "that they may become perfectly one, so that the world may know that you have sent me and *have loved them even as you have loved me*." The Father has loved us even as he has loved his Son! This means: totally, unreservedly, uniquely, intimately, and forever! We are truly "beloved sons and daughters within the beloved Son!" 7) Finally, this communion that God enables in the bosom of his Church is a real foretaste and anticipation of the unity of heaven, the "House of the Father" toward which we are all journeying. Jesus, who has come to us in our exile in this world, has made himself our divine Bridegroom, and now he goes away to prepare a place for us, so that he can come again and take us to be with him forever, espoused to him eternally in the Home of his Father (cf. Jn 14:2-3). How consoling it is to hear these words of Jesus: "Father, *I desire that they* also, whom you have given me, *may be with me* where I am, to behold my glory..." We are a gift from the Father to the Son, and the Son yearns to take us up into himself and to carry us, united with him, back into the welcoming bosom of our Father.

Now, who understands these deep aspirations of the Heart of Jesus better than his own mother? Indeed, she remained present, closer to him than any other, during the climactic hours of his Passion and into the dawning glory of his Resurrection. Therefore, she was able to witness (and to participate in) the mystery of Christ's atoning death, in which he "drew together in unity in the silence of his Heart all the lines of contradiction!" She is the Mother of Unity because she is perfectly united to the Source of all unity, Jesus Christ.

She experienced, through her compassion with Christ, in which a "sword pierced through her own soul," that Jesus is the "sign of contradiction" through which "the thoughts out of many hearts are revealed" (Luke 2:34-35). But this sign of contradiction is ultimately a sign of unity—for he unveils the divisions caused by sin only in order to destroy them in his own flesh. In this way he has "broken down the dividing wall" of separation that kept us apart and has "made us all one within himself," reconciling us to God "in one Body through the Cross" (cf. Eph 2:14-16).

By letting ourselves be drawn into this space of unity within the reconciling Heart of the Crucified and Risen Jesus, we too share in the mystery of communion that is opened at the heart of our world...at the heart of the Virgin Mary and the entire Church.

Reflection Questions:

— Mary is the Mother of Unity, joined together to the deepest aspirations of her Son, who unites all of humanity within his own Sacred Heart and draws us to the Father. Do I find in myself a yearning for this unity? Do I find in myself the desire to strive for this unity for the sake of my brothers and sisters?

— What stands out to me the most from the prayer that Jesus uttered on the night before his Passion, in which he asked for the unity of all who would believe in him?

DAY 18: A SPIRITUALITY OF COMMUNION

Jesus died "to gather together into unity all the children of God who are scattered abroad" (cf. Jn 11:51-52). Through being raised up on the Cross, he became like a divine Magnet that "draws all humanity to himself" (cf. Jn 12:32) and thus unites us both to God and to one another within the sinews of his own Sacred Heart. The inner meaning of the Gospel, therefore, is *unity*. God is a God of unity and love, of harmony and communion, of deep understanding and mutual indwelling. He lives a life of perfect intimacy for all eternity—as the Family of the Father, Son, and Holy Spirit—and he has created us to share in this intimacy.

All other elements of the New Covenant find their place within this one, all-encompassing desire of God for unity: for intimate union with each one of us as his beloved child, and for the unity of all his children as one, bound together within the embrace of his own Love. The entire life and mission of the Church derives its meaning from this innermost core of *communion*, and simply serves this communion. All of the Church's existence—her sacraments, her hierarchical structure, her life of prayer, her teaching, the witness of her saints—is simply a way of safeguarding and deepening this communion in our own lives and of drawing us more deeply into it. Finally, the mission entrusted to us as believers is simply the way that the gift of communion that we have received opens our hearts to all of our brothers and sisters—to loving, embracing, sheltering, and accompanying those who have not yet experienced the love of God and the intimacy made possible within the shelter of his Church.

Saint John Paul II understood this very well when he said that the great task of the Church in the third millennium is not some secondary "pastoral program" or some "sociological" cause, but simply **to be "the home and the school of communion."** Everything else finds its place within this. Let us quote his words in depth:

> Communion is the fruit and demonstration of that love which springs from the heart of the Eternal Father and is poured out upon us through the Spirit which Jesus gives us (cf. Rom 5:5), to

make us all "one heart and one soul" (Acts 4:32). It is in building this communion of love that the Church appears as "sacrament", as the "sign and instrument of intimate union with God and of the unity of the human race".

The Lord's words on this point are too precise for us to diminish their import. Many things are necessary for the Church's journey through history, not least in this new century; but without charity (*agape*), all will be in vain. It is again the Apostle Paul who in the *hymn to love* reminds us: even if we speak the tongues of men and of angels, and if we have faith "to move mountains", but are without love, all will come to "nothing" (cf. 1 Cor 13:2). Love is truly the "heart" of the Church, as was well understood by Saint Thérèse of Lisieux, whom I proclaimed a Doctor of the Church precisely because she is an expert in the *scientia amoris:* "I understood that the Church had a Heart and that this Heart was aflame with Love. I understood that Love alone stirred the members of the Church to act... I understood that Love encompassed all vocations, that Love was everything".

To make the Church *the home and the school of communion*: that is the great challenge facing us in the millennium which is now beginning, if we wish to be faithful to God's plan and respond to the world's deepest yearnings.

But what does this mean in practice? Here too, our thoughts could run immediately to the action to be undertaken, but that would not be the right impulse to follow. Before making practical plans, we need *to promote a spirituality of communion,* making it the guiding principle of education wherever individuals and Christians are formed, wherever ministers of the altar, consecrated persons, and pastoral workers are trained, wherever families and communities are being built up. A spirituality of communion indicates above all the heart's contemplation of the mystery of the Trinity dwelling in us, and whose light we must also be able to see shining on the face of the brothers and sisters around us. A spirituality of communion also means an ability to think of our brothers and sisters in faith within the profound unity of the Mystical Body, and therefore as "those who are a part of me". This makes us able to share their joys and sufferings, to sense their desires and attend to their needs, to offer them deep and genuine friendship. A spirituality of communion implies also the ability to see what is positive in others, to welcome it and prize it as a gift from God: not only as a gift for the brother or sister who has received it directly, but also as a "gift for me". A spirituality of communion means, finally, to know how to "make room" for our brothers and sisters, bearing "each other's burdens" (Gal 6:2). (*Novo Millennio Ineunte*, no. 42-43)

This is not the place for an in-depth analysis of this rich passage, but we do want to use it as a stepping-off point for making explicit a central theme emerging from our reflections. This theme can be expressed as follows: **a central element of making the Church the home and the school of communion, of fostering a "spirituality of communion," is recognizing and experiencing the "Marian" character of the Church.** John Paul II understood this, also, and himself spoke of how the "Marian" dimension of the Church precedes and encompasses the "Petrine" dimension (that is, the ministry of Peter and the Apostles carried on by their successors, the Pope and the bishops in communion with him). This insight has found expression in the *Catechism* itself:

In the Church this communion of men with God, in the "love [that] never ends," is the purpose which governs everything in her that is a sacramental means, tied to this passing world (1 Cor 13:18). "[The Church's] structure is totally ordered to the holiness of Christ's members. And holiness is measured according to the 'great mystery' in which the Bride responds with the gift of love to the gift of the Bridegroom." Mary goes before us all in the holiness that is the Church's mystery as "the bride without spot or wrinkle" (Eph 5:27). This is why the "Marian" dimension of the Church precedes the "Petrine." (par. 773)

What is this "Marian" dimension which lies at the heart of the Church and which governs everything else in her (even "governing" the very governing office of the hierarchy!), ordering all towards holiness? The *Catechism* is clear on this point: **it is our intimate communion with God, in which we, as bride, respond with love to the gift of the divine Bridegroom.**

In Mary we see radiantly manifested this inner heart of the Church: her breathtaking communion with God, Father, Son, and Holy Spirit. This communion flowers through the movement of mutual self-giving, in which she welcomes God entirely into herself and surrenders herself entirely to God in return. Through her loving and trust-filled openness to the Trinity, she shows forth the deepest vocation of each one of us, which is, in turn, simply our response to God's most ardent desire for us. What is this desire? It is, as Saint Andrew of Crete has beautifully said: "so that entering with the whole of his being, he may draw the whole of our being into himself and place the whole of his in us." What a breathtaking intimacy! What a blessed communion! What a wondrous unity! God wants to live in us, and to take us to live in him—and, from the heart of this unity with each one of us, also to make us one among ourselves within the single bond of his all-encompassing Love!

This is what Mary, above all, reveals to us. She helps us to experience the very heartbeat of the Trinity, burning with the desire to unite us to himself in profound love. As we saw with the image of the "prism" in a previous reflection, this central truth, this "inner sanctuary" of filial and bridal intimacy with God, is the space from which all of the Church's life spreads and toward which it is oriented as its ultimate goal.

Reflection Questions:

— Do I see how the Church's entire life is directed toward holiness, and how this holiness is ultimately nothing but loving intimacy with God?

— If I re-read the long quote from John Paul II, what particularly stands out to me?

— What does it mean that the "Marian" dimension of the Church precedes the "Petrine"?

DAY 19: HOLINESS IN THE BOSOM OF THE CHURCH

In the previous reflection we spoke about the "Marian" dimension of the Church, which is, in a way, the organizing principle that gives meaning to everything else in the life and structure of the Church within this world. We hinted at how the mystery of Mary interiorly fills and directs the very ministry of the pope, bishops, and priests. This Marian mystery, as it were, cradles the service of God's shepherds within itself, holding it within the all-enveloping reality of total receptivity to God's love, and within a profound union with him. Indeed, the apostolic ministry is ultimately ordered, too, to fostering, deepening, and protecting this reality in the hearts of all the faithful, and to spreading it to those who do not yet believe. In other words, it is oriented toward *holiness*, which is simply this reality of deep and abiding intimacy with God in love, and openness to all persons from within this love… as we let ourselves be cradled within the enveloping communion of the Body of Christ, the Church, and thus within the life of the Father, Son, and Holy Spirit.

Because of this, the unique service and office of the shepherds of the Church, from the universal ministry of the Bishop of Rome to the most hidden ministry of priest or deacon—is not in competition with the intimate, personal, and unique mystery of holiness that God seeks with each person. Rather, the two are mutually related to one another. The reality of holiness, for its part, is profoundly docile and obedient to the ministry of the shepherds of the Church—in the spirit of radical faith that participates in Mary's own total faith—since it recognizes in them the presence and activity of Christ himself. Through them it is able to discern the very contours of the eternal Father's love and the abiding reality of Christ's Incarnation, perpetuated in the world until the end of time through his mystical Body. On the other hand, the shepherds themselves, striving to serve this holiness in others, will do so ever more deeply and transparently the more they themselves are rooted in the Marian mystery of intimacy with God and docility to his slightest touch.

This, it seems to us, is precisely the "secret" of Saint John Paul II, if it can be put that way. His episcopal and papal motto is well known: "*Totus Tuus*—Totally Yours," referring to the prayer of Marian entrustment, "I am totally yours, Jesus, through Mary, and all that I have is yours." John Paul often expressed this much more simply, however, in the context of his profound and intimate filial relationship with the Mother of God. For example, in his first public message after the assassination attempt of May 13, 1981 (in which his life was saved through the intervention of the Virgin), he said: "Mary, I repeat to you today: *Totus Tuus*. I am totally yours." The depth and breadth of his apostolic ministry, and his profound, loving radiance as a man, as a priest, and as the Vicar of Christ, was the overflow of the intense communion of his heart with the Trinity. And this was a communion that matured precisely in the context of his total belonging to Mary... through his sharing in the depths of her own inner heart, her prayer, and her dispositions of faith, hope, and love. In other words, John Paul II harmonized within himself the "Marian" and "Petrine" elements of the Church so completely that they could not be separated from one another. In this way, his sanctity is a beautiful witness for all of us, revealing in a brilliant way God's intentions for each one of us and for his universal Church.

This is true because the relation between holiness and apostolic ministry (which is realized uniquely in the successors of the Apostles— the bishops and priests) is also a reality in the life of each one of us. We too, from the fullness of our experience of God's tender and unique love for us, are opened to share ourselves with others: to love as we have been loved. The discovery of our "belovedness" before God flowers in the desire to gaze upon every person in the truth of their own belovedness before him, their own unique identity as his precious child. Indeed, as our acceptance of God's love allows us to surrender ever more totally to him, letting him espouse us to himself in a breathtaking nuptial union, our hearts also expand to manifest this love for others. We become, as Saint John the Baptist said of himself, a "friend of the Bridegroom," who prepares the bride (every heart!) for the encounter with her Beloved (Jn 3:29).

Our transparency to the light and love of God for the sake of our brothers and sisters, therefore, depends upon the depths of our intimacy with the Trinity in prayer and self-surrender. It depends upon the degree to which we plunge into the "Marian heart" of the Church, sharing in Mary's experience, in her dispositions, in her contemplation, in her openness to the Spirit, in her union with Christ and, through him, with the Father.

Yes, as we have said multiple times: through Mary God opens the "space" in the bosom of the Church in which the life of each one of us can unfold in communion with the Trinity and with our brothers and sisters. This space, this "hearth of love," this "home of communion," is the deepest reality of the Church which Christ founded, and into which he invites all of humanity. Here we are enfolded in the communion of saints, in the family of redeemed humanity, in which the deepest longings and aspirations of our hearts are fulfilled—as we are made one with the Trinity, enfolded in his embrace, and one also with every person, whom we encounter most profoundly precisely in this place.

+ + +

To conclude this reflection, let us turn our gaze for a moment to one of the beautiful mysteries that we glimpsed in one of our earlier reflections: the relationship between Mary and the Holy Spirit—indeed the threefold union between the Spirit, Mary, and the Church. We could easily devote an entire week or more of thought and prayer to this topic alone. However, the essential elements are present in all that we have been saying, though the Holy Spirit's name is not made explicit every time his presence is apparent. We can summarize this way: *What the Holy Spirit is in the divine order, Mary reveals in the created order; and, further, the presence of both, Mary and the Spirit, is perpetuated in the Church.*

Saint Maximilian Kolbe explains that the Holy Spirit is, as it were, the *"uncreated* Immaculate Conception," while Mary is the *created* Immaculate Conception—in other words, the pure fruit of the love of the Father and the Son, the radiant expression of their intimacy. Indeed, we can affirm that the Holy Spirit is not only the "conception" of the love of Father and Son, but the very "womb" of the Son's eternal begetting, the "space" of the divine encounter—and himself also Beloved, a Person uniquely and infinitely loved. Thus, when the Son becomes a man, the role of the Holy Spirit becomes incarnate for him in a unique way in the person of his mother, Mary—who is irradiated wholly with the

Spirit's presence and reveals him in a particular way.

Mary is now the "womb" in which the Son's eternal begetting from the Father becomes present in time within humanity. She is also the "space," in her motherly love, through which the Son at first awakens to the outpouring gift of the Father's love and gives himself back to the Father (as we saw in our first week concerning the child's awakening to consciousness). Mary is, further, that same "womb" and "space" for each one of us, through whom we receive the love of Christ and are drawn near to him, and in whose sheltering love we are protected, nourished, and brought to maturity for the final birth into eternal life.

But this is precisely the work of the Holy Spirit! And, further, this is the work and the mystery of the Church! Therefore we are led to the profound realization that these three realities are inseparably united and work in ceaseless harmony throughout salvation history: *the Holy Spirit, Mary, and the Church*. The tender and "maternal" breath of the Holy Spirit, who is the bond of intimacy in the bosom of the Trinity—and who is also the One who draws all the children of God into unity within this world—is manifested most profoundly in the person of Mary, Virgin and Mother, and in the Church, who perpetuates this mystery in each one of us until the end of time.[1]

Reflection Questions:

1. It is significant that the two "bookends" of Mary's life as presented in Scripture are both experiences of the Holy Spirit: the *Annunciation* and *Pentecost*. In the first, Mary welcomes the overshadowing of the Holy Spirit and through him conceives the Son within her womb, to bring him forth into the world as a man. In the second, Mary receives the overshadowing of the Spirit again, this time for the sake of the birth of Christ's mystical Body, the Church. Indeed, this overshadowing of the Holy Spirit continues in the Church whenever the "Marian" spirit—or rather the presence and love of Mary—opens our hearts to welcome the Spirit anew and to consent to the Trinity's Love which he makes present.

Indeed, we can also note that the climax of Mary's union with Christ is also mediated by the Spirit, and is an expression of her own union with the Spirit: her reception of the blood and water flowing from the side of the Crucified Christ, at the foot of whose Cross Mary stands in faith and love. As Saint John writes in his first Letter, it is not only blood and water which pour forth from Christ's Heart, but "the Spirit, the water, and the blood" (1 Jn 5:8), and Mary is there to welcome all three and to carry them within herself...present and active in the heart of Mother Church until the consummation of all things.

— *Do I see how the depths of my intimacy with God in prayer is the direct source of the fruitfulness of my life for the good of my brothers and sisters?*

— *Is there something within me that holds me back from opening myself totally to God's gift, and from surrendering myself completely into his hands?*

— *What is my response to the words drawing attention to the deep relationship between the Holy Spirit, Mary, and the Church?*

DAY 20: THE BELOVED DISCIPLE

We said in our previous reflection that Saint John Paul II in a profound way unified in himself the "Marian" holiness and the "Petrine" ministry of the Church. He bore within his heart and his life the interior, contemplative mystery of ineffable intimacy with God (the mystery of Mary), and also the external, apostolic role of shepherd and evangelist (the mystery of Peter and the Apostles). This union of the distinct yet complementary dimensions of the Church, however, is not something new, and it certainly does not apply only to John Paul II. Rather, it comes about wherever authentic holiness flowers. Whenever a human heart plunges into the inner mystery of the Church—the "hearth" of her reality as Bride and Body of Christ, which "unifies all the lines of contradiction"—this harmonization takes place.

This unification is revealed in the very events recounted by the Word of God itself: in the life of Christ and his Apostles. There we can discern the structure and mystery of the Church symbolized in its radiant unity, in the white-hot light that stands at the origin of her existence in this world. We have seen how Mary "bears" the entire universal Church within her own unique "Yes," within the mystery of her communion with the Trinity. We can thus affirm that the "dimension" of the Church revealed in her is indeed the primary and all-enveloping dimension, in which the others find their place and which they serve. The dimension of the Church entrusted to Peter and the Apostles—and indeed to the other disciples whom Christ forms and sends out in his name—itself expresses, serves, and exists only to shelter this Marian mystery. Nonetheless, while this mystery applies to all, there is a certain Apostle who manifests to us in a particularly clear way the union of these two dimensions: *it is the beloved disciple, John the Evangelist.*

We spoke earlier of how Mary's whole existence is cradled in the arms of perfect Love, and how her whole life springs forth from her awareness of being totally and forever loved by God. In other words, her life is contained within, and flows from, her abiding *belovedness* before God. Indeed, we saw that Mary's very name is ultimately "beloved." It is significant therefore, that, in his Gospel, John the Evangelist never gives his own name. He always simply refers to himself as "the disciple whom Jesus loved" as if this were his true identity...which, of course, it is. Through experiencing the tender love of Jesus, John's eyes and heart are opened to the infinite love of the heavenly Father—and therefore to discovering his own unique identity within the gaze of God. He experiences, like Mary does, the all-enveloping and cradling arms of perfect Love, and he is able to entrust himself entirely to this Love.

This is the deep significance of those words describing his position at the Last Supper: "One of the disciples, the one whom Jesus loved, was lying close to the bosom of Jesus." Through resting against the bosom of Christ, John is able to hear and feel the heartbeat of the Incarnate Son of God, and in him indeed to feel pulsating the entire Mystery of the Holy Trinity. In other words, he rests at the very Wellspring of Love, at the Origin of the undivided Light, before it is refracted in diverse colors. By his proximity to the heart of Christ, therefore, John lets himself be introduced into the central mystery of the Church (this mystery lived so intensely by Mary!); he lets himself be taken up into the intimate life of the Father, Son, and Holy Spirit.

When Jesus offers himself in the Holy Eucharist, John is there, against his breast, welcoming this torrent of overflowing Love. When Jesus opens his Heart to his disciples and prays to the Father in their presence, asking that all who believe will be one with the very unity of the Trinity, John is there, intimately close to his Beloved. His intimacy with Christ allows him to sense, and to share in, the Son's own intimacy with his Father. John is very explicit about this when he writes his Gospel, for two of the most central passages of the entire book are these: "No one has ever seen God; the only-begotten Son, who is in the bosom of the Father, he has made him known" (Jn 1:18) and, "One of the disciples, whom Jesus loved, was lying close to the bosom of Jesus" (Jn 13:23). In a word, by reposing against the bosom of Jesus, the beloved disciple allows himself to be taken up to share in the Son's own filial union with the Father, his resting in the Father's bosom...to share in the Son's own belovedness and his repose in the cradling arms of the Trinity's perfect Love.

And this intimacy, this awareness of being cradled in the arms of Love—a Love which is undying, total, and constant, and which nothing can overcome—allows John to remain close to Christ even through the darkness and anguish of his Passion. He alone of all the Apostles stands at the foot of the Cross, at the side of Mary, present to the Crucified Jesus in love, obedience, and tender compassion. In this place, beholding the Son of God giving himself to "the very end" (Jn 13:1) out of love for humanity, John witnesses the complete revelation of Divine Love, unveiled in the naked and suffering body of Jesus Christ. And here, indeed, he finds himself sharing in the "Marian" heart of the Church—for, as the Church Fathers have said, the Church is born from the wounded side of the Redeemer just as Eve was born from the side of Adam in the beginning. Therefore the Cross is both a birth and, yes, a marriage, where the bridal Church is united totally to her divine Bridegroom on what has been called the "marriage-bed" of the Cross.

Here John stands, close to the Virgin Mary, witnessing the outpouring love of the heavenly Bridegroom, and the love of the Father which this gift reveals. While abiding in this place, further, he hears those awesome words which Christ addresses, first to Mary, and then to him: "Woman, behold your son... Behold, your mother..." He then writes that, after this, "the disciple took her into all that was his own" (Jn 19:26-27). He welcomes this woman, the Mother of Jesus who has become the Mother of the Church, into his own home, into the intimacy of his life. Through this, he is entrusted in a special way with "caring" for the mystery of the Church, as well as, indeed, letting himself be enfolded in the Church's deep mystery, which touches him through the person of Mary. Finally, he is the first of the Apostles to recognize and believe in the Resurrection of Christ...this victory of perfect Love over all darkness, estrangement, and death.

He himself, racing Peter to the tomb on Easter morning, arrives first, but, in humble reverence for the office entrusted to Peter, he allows him to enter the tomb first. Yet it is the beloved disciple who first believes. He is also present on the lake when Peter invites the Apostles to join him in going fishing, and John recognizes the Lord from afar after the miraculous catch of fish. The burning ardor and contemplative love of his heart allows him to see and know Christ with profound clarity and deep intimacy. And yet this very seeing is not his own prerogative, a merely private seeing, but is open wide as a gift for the sake of all the Apostles, for the good of the entire Church...flowing out and returning to that throbbing heartbeat of intimacy at the heart of the Church where he ceaselessly abides.

Therefore, when Peter is in deep conversation with Jesus on the shore, asked by the Lord three times, "Do you love me?" and receiving in response the invitation, "Tend my sheep...Feed my lambs," John is present, humbly *following them*. Yes, John knows his place, he knows what it means to abide at the heart of the Church in authentic holiness. He knows the intimacy that Christ has gifted him with—an intimacy destined for every individual person—an intimacy that he seeks to serve with his entire existence. And so he "follows" in the footsteps of Jesus and Peter, humbly placing his feet in the path that they mark out, while also offering the unrepeatable service of his own burning contemplative love and the gift of his life.

Here, indeed, he is unifying the "Marian" and "Petrine" dimensions of the Church, in the dimension that he himself has experienced: the "Johannine" dimension. This is probably the meaning of Jesus' mysterious words of response, when Peter turns around and sees John following them, and then asks: "What about this man, Lord?" Jesus replies, "What is it to you if I desire him to abide until I come? Follow me" (cf. Jn 20 and 21). John makes clear that Jesus' words do not mean that the beloved disciple himself will live until Christ's second coming. What then do these words mean mean? They seems to mean that the "spirit" of the beloved disciple—this profound abiding in the contemplative heart of the Church in intimacy with the Trinity—will endure until the end of time.

Indeed, it is precisely this spirit of the "beloved disciple" which is offered to every one of us, who are each a beloved disciple of Christ. We are enfolded in the arms of perfect Love just as John, just as Mary, and we are invited to welcome this Love and to surrender to it totally. In this way we too will abide in this burning Hearth of Love at the center of the Church, sharing in and perpetuating this Mystery until the end of time.

Reflection Questions:

— Can I relate to the beloved disciple's experience of leaning against the bosom of Christ? Have I experienced the reality of being cradled within the arms of Love, and gazed upon with the loving eyes of God?

— Do I understand how the desire to "follow" in the footsteps of Peter is an act of love for the Church and a service of her unity?

— Do I see how my own most intimate relationship with God is also important for all of my brothers and sisters? Can I glimpse how I personally share in the "spirit" of contemplative love and intimacy that will "abide" in the Church until the end of time?

DAY 21: AT THE HEART OF THE PASCHAL MYSTERY

Our reflections on the beloved disciple have led us, perhaps unexpectedly, right to the heart of the meaning of Marian consecration, or, as John Paul II preferred to call it, "entrustment to Mary." How so? Because the beloved disciple John is precisely the first person to entrust himself to Mary in this way...at the foot of the Cross of Jesus. This is not just our idea, but the explanation of the pope himself. Let's read his words. Indeed, in this reflection, let us try to allow him to speak for himself, meditating on his own vision of what occurred at the foot of the Cross:

It can also be said that these same words ["Behold, your son"] fully show the reason for the Marian dimension of the life of Christ's disciples. This is true not only of John, who at that hour stood at the foot of the Cross together with his Master's Mother, but it is also true of every disciple of Christ, of every Christian. The Redeemer entrusts his mother to the disciple, and at the same time he gives her to him as his mother. Mary's motherhood, which becomes man's inheritance, is a gift: a gift which Christ himself makes personally to every individual. The Redeemer entrusts Mary to John because he entrusts John to Mary. At the foot of the Cross there begins that special entrusting of humanity to the Mother of Christ, which in the history of the Church has been practiced and expressed in different ways. The same Apostle and Evangelist, after reporting the words addressed by Jesus on the Cross to his Mother and to himself, adds: "And from that hour the disciple took her to his own home" (Jn 19:27). This statement certainly means that the role of son was attributed to the disciple and that he assumed responsibility for the Mother of his beloved Master. And since Mary was given as a mother to him personally, the statement indicates, even though indirectly, everything expressed by the intimate relationship of a child with its mother. And all of this can be included in the word "entrusting." Such entrusting is the response to a person's love, and in particular to the love of a mother. (*Redemptoris Mater*, no. 45)

In other words, in the unique existence of the Apostle John, God commences the "entrustment" of all humanity into Mary's maternal care, and, in turn, her intimate relationship with every disciple of Christ. Why does Christ inaugurate this movement of entrustment with one single individual—John—rather than explicitly offering Mary as the mother of all humanity? The pope gives us the reason for this too:

> Of the essence of motherhood is the fact that it concerns the person. Motherhood always establishes a unique and unrepeatable relationship between two people: between mother and child and between child and mother. Even when the same woman is the mother of many children, her personal relationship with each one of them is of the very essence of motherhood. For each child is generated in a unique and unrepeatable way, and this is true both for the mother and for the child. Each child is surrounded in the same way by that maternal love on which are based the child's development and coming to maturity as a human being.

> It can be said that motherhood "in the order of grace" preserves the analogy with what "in the order of nature" characterizes the union between mother and child. In the light of this fact it becomes easier to understand why in Christ's testament on Golgotha his Mother's new motherhood is expressed in the singular, in reference to one man: "Behold your son." (Ibid.)

Yes, though Mary is the mother of all, she is not the mother of a generic or anonymous multitude, but *of each unique and precious child of God*. From the heart of her filial and spousal intimacy with the Trinity, her heart is open to see, to love, and to welcome every human person. Indeed, this is her ardent desire: to enfold us in her own maternal love, revealing to us anew in this way the love that we first glimpsed as children, and indeed, to draw us still further, ever deeper into the immensity of the Trinity's perfect Love which alone can satisfy the thirst of our hearts.

As John Paul II concludes: "For every Christian, for every human being, Mary is the one who first 'believed,' and precisely with her faith as Spouse and Mother she wishes to act upon all those who entrust themselves to her as her children. And it is well known that the more her children persevere and progress in this attitude, the nearer Mary leads them to the 'unsearchable riches of Christ' (Eph. 3:8)" (no. 46).

This immersion in the "unsearchable riches of Christ" through persevering and progressing in the attitude of childlike belonging to Mary...this is precisely what we have been saying in our previous reflections about the heart of holiness. But why did this entrustment to Mary occur at the foot of the Cross, and not somewhere else? Because it is precisely upon the Cross that Jesus manifests the full splendor of Divine Love, this Love that radiates through his total self-giving and pours forth from his opened Heart. This is the space in which the Wellspring unleashes its torrents right at the heart of the aridity of our world, and where the Light sends forth its rays in the midst of creation's darkness.

Christ has drawn near to us through the Cross and he gives himself to us here in love. The mystery of Jesus' Passion and Resurrection did not happen once "merely in the past" in such a way that it is consigned to ancient history. Rather, these sacred events have an eternal significance—through which eternity poured forth into our world—and themselves have been taken up into the heart of eternity in order to be made present in each moment of time. This eternal significance is made especially present in the Church's sacraments, especially the Eucharist. Indeed, the mystery of Calvary is made fully present at every Mass. When we kneel before the elevated Host and chalice, we are side by side with Mary and John at the foot of the Cross. When we receive Holy Communion, we are welcoming the healing and transforming gift that pours forth always from the Heart of the Crucified Redeemer.

And yet we are not only sharing in the mystery of the Passion—witnesses of Crucified Love that gives itself to the very end—but we are sharing already in the mystery of the Resurrection. This is because the One who comes to us and gives us his Body and Blood is not the mortal Christ, in the weak temporal existence he had before his Passion, but the Risen One whose entire being has been immersed in the fullness of the Trinity's life, and who from this fullness is able to communicate himself freely to all. Yes, in rising from the tomb Jesus has "unified all the lines of contradiction" within his Risen Body; he has made all of the moments of his earthly life present in the heart of God's eternity. And from this eternity he makes himself unceasingly present within the passing flow of our world. When we allow ourselves to be drawn to the space of his self-giving, therefore, eternity intersects with time, and we already taste the fullness of eternal life that awaits us at the end of time.

Mary simply wants to help us to abide here, at the heart of her own life, at the heart of the life of the Church, where the Paschal Mystery of Christ is unceasingly at work within the midst of creation. She wants to hold us in the shelter of her love, and thus to help us experience ever more deeply the enveloping Love of God. She wants to shelter and uphold us as we, too, accompany Christ on his passage from Holy Thursday to Easter Sunday. Here she wants to help us to drink from the Wellspring of Salvation which is Jesus' Crucified Heart, and to let ourselves be encompassed within the enduring embrace of his Risen Body, which, sharing in the very universal proportions of the Trinity, cradles the entire universe within itself.

Reflection Questions:

— Do I recognize and experience Mary's unrepeatable maternal love for me, in my own unique existence? Or do I feel like an "anonymous" member of the mass of humanity?

— What is my understanding and experience of the Paschal Mystery of Jesus' Passion and Resurrection? How might I experience more deeply the light of Love pouring forth from the self-giving of Christ?

WEEK 4

THE ROSE THAT HEALS US AMONG OUR THORNS

DAY 22: THE INNER OPENNESS OF LOVE

Let us begin this reflection by recalling what we spoke of at the end of the last week. We will do this, not with our own words, but by again quoting Saint John Paul II:

> On the Cross Christ said: "Woman, behold, your son!" With these words he opened in a new way his Mother's heart. A little later, the Roman soldier's spear pierced the side of the Crucified One. That pierced Heart became a sign of the redemption achieved through the death of the Lamb of God.
>
> The Immaculate Heart of Mary, opened with the words "Woman, behold, your son!", is spiritually united with the Heart of her Son opened by the soldier's spear. Mary's Heart was opened by the same love for man and for the world with which Christ loved man and the world, offering himself for them on the Cross, until the soldier's spear struck that blow.
>
> Consecrating the world to the Immaculate Heart of Mary means drawing near, through the Mother's intercession, to the very Fountain of life that sprang from Golgotha. This Fountain pours forth unceasingly redemption and grace. In it reparation is made continually for the sins of the world. It is a ceaseless source of new life and holiness.
>
> Consecrating the world to the Immaculate Heart of the Mother means returning beneath the Cross of the Son. It means consecrating this world to the pierced Heart of the Savior, bringing it back to the very source of its Redemption. Redemption is always greater than man's sin and the "sin of the world." The power of the Redemption is infinitely superior to the whole range of evil in man and the world.
>
> The Heart of the Mother is aware of this, more than any other heart in the whole universe, visible and invisible. And so she calls us. She not only calls us to be converted: she calls us to accept her motherly help to return to the source of Redemption.
>
> Through her union with the pierced Heart of Jesus, Mary's heart,

too, shares in a universal love, in a love of complete openness, in the love of God that is boundless in its depth and breadth. Mary's love, we said, is universal not by embracing an anonymous mass of humanity, but by being tenderly and uniquely open to each unrepeatable individual, who can be truly seen, known, and understood only within the light of God's all-enveloping Love. Yes, through her abiding closeness to her Son, through her total surrender to him, Mary becomes transparent to the tenderness of God's own Love, to the radiance of his loving gaze which is fixed unceasingly upon each one of us.

When we entrust ourselves to Mary, we are giving her permission to exercise this love fully and freely in our life. Indeed, we are consenting to allow her to draw us to the place where we most deeply desire to be, but where we cannot go on our own. We are allowing her to take us by the hand and to draw us with her close to the Heart of Jesus. "Consecrating" ourselves "to the Immaculate Heart of Mary," John Paul said, "means drawing near, through the Mother's intercession, to the very Fountain of life that sprang from Golgotha." It means going "back to the very source of Redemption."

Yes, Mary yearns to draw us to the open Heart of her Son, where his openness meets our openness, his vulnerability meets our vulnerability, his thirst meets our thirst. In this encounter, Divine Love can touch us in the most intimate way, healing, liberating, and transforming us in the places of our deepest need. Then the mystery of that Wellspring that pours forth from the Cross will lead us, with absolute certainty, to the radiant light and the unbreakable joy of the Resurrection.

During this fourth and final full week of our preparation, we are going to focus in a special way on the inner dispositions of the heart of Mary—and her role in fashioning these dispositions within us as well. We have said that our entrustment to her is a matter of placing the care of our life in her hands, our heart in her heart, our "Yes" within her own perfect "Yes." This allows her to enfold our life, at its every moment, within her own motherly presence, and to fashion within our hearts her own most intimate desires and dispositions. Thus, just as she loved Jesus so deeply and intimately throughout her life, she will enable us to do the same, in our own circumstances, in the unique story of our life which unfolds within the loving providence of God.

To begin, let us quote one of the earliest and most influential writings on Mary from the early Church. This will provide a basis around which our reflections will turn. It comes from the pen of Saint Irenaeus, in his book *Against Heresies*. He draws a parallel between the Virgin Mary, on the one hand, and the Virgin Eve, on the other:

> In accordance with this design, Mary the Virgin is found obedient, saying, "Behold the handmaid of the Lord; be it done unto me according to thy word" (Lk 1:38). But Eve was disobedient; for she did not obey when as yet she was a virgin. Even though Eve had Adam as a husband, she was still a virgin. For "they were both naked in paradise and they were unashamed" (Gn 2:25) since they were created a short time previously to become adults, and only then did they begin to multiply. Having become disobedient, she was made the cause of death, both to herself and to the entire human race. So also did Mary, having a man betrothed to her, and being nevertheless a virgin, by yielding obedience, become the cause of salvation, both to herself and the whole human race.
>
> And on this account does the law call a woman betrothed to a man, the wife of him who had betrothed her, although she was as yet a virgin; thus indicating a parallelism in reference back from Mary to Eve. For what was tied together once cannot be loosened except by untying the knot in reverse order so that the second knot be dissolved by untying it first and the first knot be dissolved by untying it second. In this way the former knots become canceled by a latter untying, and the latter ties are set free by the formed untying. ... In this way the Lord declared that the first will be the last and the last first (cf. Mt 19:30).[ii]

This has been quoted often in a shortened form: "The knot of Eve's disobedience was untied through Mary's obedience." Mary is, therefore, truly the "Untier of Knots," as we see in the beautiful image that has recently become popular. Through her trusting acceptance of God's loving invitation—through her wholehearted obedience—she allows God to begin untying the knots of sin which bind our hearts.

We immediately see in the above quote two primary dispositions that characterize the heart of Mary: *obedience* and *virginity*. We can add a third: *poverty*. Thus we see in her the wellspring of what tradition has come to call the "evangelical counsels," the threefold form of surrender that religious and consecrated persons vow when they bind themselves to God. **Mary is truly the obedient, chaste, and poor one, who in her complete openness of heart welcomes all that God gives to her at every moment, and surrenders herself entirely to him in return. And precisely through her loving openness, God is able to unite her to himself in the most profound intimacy, binding her to himself as a daughter, spouse, and mother.**

But why talk of the evangelical counsels, if these are the prerogatives of religious persons, and not for the rest of the faithful? The simple answer is that they are *not* the prerogatives of religious, but are intended for all—though their literal expressions are often unique to religious. Indeed, they are the very *inner form* of holiness that is realized uniquely in the life of each individual person. All love is inherently obedient, chaste, and poor, as we will soon see...and these three realities are ultimately only one. They are simply different aspects of a single interior disposition of the heart—which in turn is manifested in all the external details of our life. **This reality is openness is trusting acceptance and loving self-gift, which blossoms in an intimacy with the Beloved...an intimacy that is, in turn, inherently fruitful.**

When Mary, as our tender mother, invites us to entrust ourselves to her, it is because she wants to draw us close to her heart and to begin untying the knots which constrict the flow of love in our life. She wants, indeed, to draw us into the flow of love that ever passes between her heart and the Heart of her Son—a circulation of immense tenderness between Lover and Beloved, totally open in radiant trust, confidence, and shared joy.

This is what we mean by the dispositions of obedience, poverty, and chastity, which shine so brightly in the lives of Jesus and Mary; they are simply this openness of love, and the bond of communion that knits their hearts together in an unbreakable unity. This is the bond of love which alone can untie to bonds of sin which keep us closed in upon ourselves, wrought up in anxiety and fear in the confines of our broken hearts.

Reflection Questions:

— Do I grasp the way in which love is "openness" to another, and sin is "closedness"? Can I reflect on the difference between Mary and Eve, precisely as an attitude of openness or closedness to God and his Love?

— *Whenever the "knot" of love between us and God is severed through deliberately turning away from him in sin, we inevitably find ourselves "knotted" to other things in his place. However, our knittedness to God is true freedom, but our binding to created things in sin is unfreedom. Do I experience this?*

DAY 23: UNIFIED IN LOVE

In yesterday's reflection we began meditating on the innermost dispositions of the heart of Mary—and of the Heart of her Son. While we will not be able to speak about all the depth and richness of these dispositions (even if we had more space to do so), we will try to focus on the central ones, those which "unite" all the others in a profound harmony and simplicity. This, indeed, is a primary trait of Mary's heart, as of her whole existence: simplicity and unity. She allowed her whole life to unfold in a deep spontaneity, a deep and unquestioning assent to the mysterious workings of God's Love within her and around her. She did not, in other words, create unnecessary and unrealistic "problems" for herself, which would cloud and confuse the pristine purity of her relationship with God. Rather, she welcomed in radical openness the joys and challenges which her real, concrete life brought, and, above all, the One who came to her unceasingly in, through, and beyond all things.

What was the cause of Mary's interior simplicity and unity? It is precisely what we spoke of last time. She is united *within* herself precisely because she is always open *beyond* herself…in complete loving dependence upon Another, who sustains her at every instant. This is because her unity, as intimate and interior as it may be, could not possibly be the result of her own efforts or the autonomy of her being "closed in on itself." Rather, her heart—just like the heart of every human person—is inherently *relational*, meaning that it comes from, depends upon, and is ordered toward relationship with another. When we live in such relationship, then we are spontaneously unified, not only with the other, but also within ourselves. In a word, to go *within* ourselves truly is simultaneously to go *beyond* ourselves toward the God who loves us and sustains us, and vice versa.

Saint Augustine had this experience of discovering God in his inmost being—and of discovering himself only by transcending himself toward God. He spoke about how, as a result of sin, he experienced the profound "fragmentation" of his being, in which he lived in a kind of exile on the surface of himself, immersed in created things, but far from both God and from his own authentic truth:

> Late have I loved you, O Beauty ever ancient, ever new, late have I loved you! You were within me, but I was outside, and it was there that I searched for you. In my unloveliness I plunged into the lovely things which you created. You were with me, but I was not with you. Created things kept me from you, yet if they had not been in you, they would not have been at all. You called, you shouted, and you broke through my deafness. You flashed, you shone, and you dispelled my blindness. You breathed your fragrance on me, I drew in breath, and now I pant for you. I have tasted you, now I hunger and thirst for more. You touched me, and I burned for your peace.[iii]

These words of Saint Augustine vividly paint a picture of our own experience, don't they? We yearn to be with God, to live within and from our own authentic identity as his beloved child, and yet we find ourselves "far away," immersed in created things. These things themselves speak of God, but only as an echo. They reveal him, but they also conceal him—like a veil through which a light dimly filters through, a light which will be seen in its full brightness only when the veil is removed.

And indeed, our struggle is not only that our desire for God encounters resistance through our fragmentation among created things, our exile from the sanctuary of our heart. Our struggle perhaps also consists in the fact that our heart itself is afraid and filled with shame, that we are not in touch with our desire for God, that we do not know his immense love for us and therefore cannot unconditionally entrust ourselves to this Love. Yes, even in the sanctuary of the heart we encounter the wounds of our sins and the brokenness that we carry within us. The external expressions of our flight from the face of God bubble up from this deep place of insecurity—a compensation for our fear, a feverish seeking for comfort or consolation in a place where it cannot truly be found.

This is the inheritance that we have received because of original sin. For we see that Adam and Eve, before their sin, were unified in child-like simplicity before the face of their heavenly Father. They were united within themselves because they were totally open to God, abiding in complete trusting dependence upon him. They were able, as we saw in the first week, to rejoice in a childlike playfulness and in a peaceful repose—for they allowed God's Love to cradle and shelter them within itself. This openness to God, this love and trust that lived in their hearts as his gift, was like the "cord" that bound together all the elements of their existence in a beautiful harmony. They were united to God, and therefore they were unified within themselves, they were in communion with each other, and, finally, in communion with the whole of creation.

In a sense we can say that their childlike openness before the Father was like the chain of a rosary, which holds all the beads together. But when the chain is broken, the beads are no longer bound together and scatter all over the place. When Adam and Eve rested in the Father's Love, when they consented to receive their existence from him at every moment as a pure gift, all was as it should be, radiant in beauty and harmony. Their childlike union with him allowed them to be "naked" before each other "without shame," and allowed their very cultivating of the Garden to be, not a burdensome task, but a form of playful responsibility, or responsible play (in other words, play that is a fitting *response* to the gift and invitation of God ever given). Further, their childlikeness was able to flower freely in a spousal union (both with God and with each other) and in the transparent fruitfulness of parenthood.

This openness, this harmony, is precisely what we indicated in the last reflection as the "inner form of love" which is *one* and yet *threefold*: obedience, poverty, and chastity. Adam and Eve were **obedient** because they trustingly welcomed all as a gift of the Father's Love, and lived in the concreteness of their life according to the inner meaning of this gift. They were **poor**, not with a poverty of lack but of abundance, because they did not grasp anything as "mine," but shared all in the "We" of loving communion; thus, while possessing nothing, they had all things. They were **chaste** because their hearts were completely open to God and to another another, in which each lived from the inner truth of the heart and looked upon this inner truth in the other; in a word, their every glance was a glance of love, a heart-to-heart communication in which "I" and "You" met within the Love of God that bound them together.

This is the "knot" of loving intimacy for which God made us, the radiant communion that alone can satisfy the longings of our hearts.

But as we know, Adam and Eve were asked to freely consent to this state, to the gift God gave to them—to set their seal upon it by choosing God alone, freely and completely. In other words, they were asked to "bind" themselves to God through an act of total surrender, choosing to be forevermore his beloved children (and spouses!), united to him in an enduring union of love and belonging. The "test" of this consent came in the form of the "fruit of the tree of the knowledge of good and evil," which represents the opposite of childlike belonging to God: it represents "adult" autonomy, the will to "go one's own way" without relying upon another. It represents the desire to create from within oneself what can only come as a gift from without, and to safeguard in isolation what can only be sheltered within the loving arms of God.

Adam and Eve—tempted by the serpent's lies that God was not a loving Father, but an arbitrary and demanding Taskmaster—turned away from obedience to God, from the openness of love that was poor and chaste, and severed the bond of intimacy with God. They were still, it is true, cradled unceasingly within the Love of God, still sustained by him at every moment, but now their hearts had collapsed in upon themselves. They covered over their nakedness in fear and shame, and "hid from the face of the Lord God among the trees of the garden." The "knot" of intimacy was broken, and yet their hearts still yearned, still reached out for something to satisfy their innate thirst, which no sin or infidelity could destroy. The frays of this broken bond were therefore tied together in the knot of sin, which knitted their life to the world in a disordered movement of pride, possessiveness, and lust—which are the direct contrary of the loving movement of obedience, poverty, and chastity.[2]

---

2. To see the "threefold concupiscence," as the Church calls it, see Gen 3:6, and 1 Jn 2:15-17. These are the three modes in which the human heart, turning away from God, is tempted to grasp for created things in an unhealthy way. We can summarize such a movement with three "p" words: pride, possessiveness, and pleasure-seeking. Jesus and Mary, by living sinless lives of obedience, poverty, and chastity within this world, healed in themselves the wounds of our hearts and opened the path for us to rediscover pure love once again. We see this, for example in the threefold temptation of Jesus in the desert (cf. Mt 4:1-11), in which he overcomes the devil precisely in the place where he tempted Adam and Eve, and thus shows himself to be the "new Adam" who begins a new creation where the first creation was corrupted.

Reflection Questions:

— *When in my life have I experienced the way that going **beyond** myself to another also unifies me **within** myself? For example, encountering beauty in nature, art, or music, or loving another person or experiencing their love?*

— *Do I see how obedience, poverty, and chastity are simply expressions of trusting openness in love? Can I reflect more deeply on each of these and try to apply them in my own life?*

— *To do this, I can ask: What obstacles are there within me to obedience...to poverty...to chastity? On the other hand, what opportunities or gifts is God offering to me in each of these areas?*

DAY 24: KNITTED TOGETHER IN HER WOMB

In the light of what we said in the last reflection, we can revisit our quote from Saint Irenaeus with much deeper understanding. We recall that its central point was that Mary is the "New Eve" whose obedience unties the knot tied by the first Eve's disobedience. We saw how this obedience is also inseparable from the reality of Mary's virginity (or chastity) and her poverty—that is, her unified childlike openness before God and his Love. But perhaps the most important thing that we realized in our reflections is that Mary not only "unties" the knot of sin which binds us in a disordered way to this world, and to our own fears, wounds, and compulsions, but that she "ties" the knot of loving and trust-filled intimacy with God once again.

This is what she desires to do for each one of us, and she does so by helping us to open up the wounds of our inner hearts—and all the struggles, hopes, joys, and sorrows of our life—to the loving touch of our heavenly Father once again. It is then God who—through the openness that Mary has helped to foster, and the "Yes" that she sustains within her own "Yes"—knits us to himself in breathtaking intimacy. This movement of "re-opening" our hearts to God's touch is the core of our process of healing and transformation.

It is the way in which we refuse to hide like Adam and Eve after their sin, taking refuge among the "trees of the garden" and covering over our nakedness in shame. Rather, it is our willingness to open our nakedness to God's loving gaze, not to be condemned, rejected, or abused, but simply to allow ourselves to be loved. For this is all that God desires to do...to be allowed to love us and to reveal to us the truth of his own loving gaze. As we said, this is the simple heart of all prayer: looking into the loving gaze of the One who always looks upon us. In this mutual encounter of looks we will find that, while God's Heart aches at seeing our brokenness, our sin, our woundedness—which keeps us from experiencing his Love and intimacy with him—his Heart even more rejoices at the unique and unspeakable beauty that he sees in us.

When we allow this gaze to continually, gently shine its light into our own experience of life, gradually we will come "home" to the authentic truth of our being before God. We will return to that space where we are, in truth, pure relationship with God as his beloved child. Bathed in the light of his tender gaze, we will be able to entrust ourselves entirely into his hands, placing our life unreservedly in his care. Indeed, we will thirst to belong to him, to abandon ourselves to him, and to give our whole being in love for our Beloved. This is because we will find ourselves less and less constricted by our fears, our shame, and the disordered movements of our sin. It is also because, as this "knot" of brokenness is gradually dissolved by God's touch, another "knot" is made ever firmer: the bond of love that knits our heart to God in profound intimacy.

This knot of intimacy will become ever stronger as our gaze encounters God's gaze, as his gaze indeed awakens and sustains our own loving gaze in return. Just as in the case of natural human love, our hearts will communicate through our eyes, and this communication will become a mutual sharing of what is most interior to each one of us. Through his loving gaze, God welcomes all that we are into himself, cradling it within the recesses of his own Divine Heart. He holds our often aching and bleeding heart within his tender Mercy; he holds us even in our sin, and wants only the "Yes" which will allow him to consume our sins like a speck of dust in a blazing fire. And then fear gives way to desire, and shame gives way to the longing to be seen and known.

Indeed, our experience of being seen, known, and loved opens the way for us to see, know, and love in return, glimpsing in faith the ineffable Beauty of the Trinity. It opens a space in us where God can communicate himself, where he can share with us what is most interior and intimate to him—these ineffable riches of his divine life and love which he thirsts to pour out into us. This glimpse of God's Beauty cannot but stir in our hearts a profound thirst—a thirst for ever deeper union with him and the ever deeper gift of ourselves to him, and also the desire that all may know this Beautiful One and experience his ravishing joy.

This loving and contemplative gaze lies at the heart of Mary's existence, both in time and, now, in eternity. She is immersed in the loving gaze of the Trinity, and the light of his gaze irradiates her so purely and totally that it passes directly, without any obstruction, into us. Indeed, in a way she "magnifies" this Light, as she said in her *Magnificat*. She reveals, in her own unique existence, in her closeness to us as a daughter of Eve and yet as the new and sinless Eve, the beauty of God's never-failing Love. To place ourselves in her heart, to let her cradle us in her maternal love, is therefore to let ourselves be sheltered in the furnace of the Trinity's presence that burns with white-hot intensity in her bosom.

The first Eve became "the mother of all the living," but only after she had already experienced in herself the fracture of sin, the state of separation from God. All of the children of humanity experience the effects of that choice of disobedience, since we have a nature that, while still beautiful, is fractured and broken. What we receive when we are conceived in our mother's womb is both beautiful and broken. This is because part we receive from Adam and Eve (mediated through our parents), a nature already marred by sin. The other part—and the more intimate, more profound, and more authentic reality—we receive directly from the hand of God. This is clear in two phrases from the Psalms, which seem almost to contradict each other, but in truth express these two aspects: **our inheritance of a fallen human nature, on the one hand, and yet, on the other, the very "fingerprint" of God that lies, untouched and pure, in the "virgin-point" of our inmost being where we are his unique image and likeness.**

The two phrases from the Psalms are as follows. The first comes from the famous penitential Psalm 51, which expresses David's lament and contrition after his sin of adultery with Bathsheba:

Behold, I was brought forth in iniquity,
and in sin did my mother conceive me. (v. 5)

He acknowledges, in other words, the inheritance of "iniquity" and "sin" that marks his existence from the very moment of his conception. However, he also immediately speaks of the deeper reality of the "inward being" and the "secret heart" in which God invites him to truth and wisdom, to a bond of love that surpasses his brokenness and indeed opens the pathway to healing:

Behold, you desire truth in the inward being;
therefore teach me wisdom in my secret heart. (v. 5-6)

The second Psalm we want to look at, which approaches this reality from the other side—from the side of what comes from the touch and the "fingerprint" of God, is Psalm 139:

> For you formed my inward parts,
> you knitted me together in my mother's womb.
> I praise you, for I am wondrously made.
> Wonderful are your works! (v. 13-14a)

How beautiful are these verses, in which the Psalmist praises God for the unique and intricate work of his own being! We can make these words our own, since each one of us has been "knitted together in our mother's womb" with such care, such tenderness, and such love that it is as if were are the only person God has ever made. To try to make contact with this space of God's creative action, with this foundation of our existence in our mother's womb, is indeed to enter into the perspective of God's own loving gaze, as we see in the succeeding verses:

> You know me right well;
> my frame was not hidden from you,
> when I was being made in secret,
> intricately wrought in the depths of the womb.
> Your eyes beheld my unformed substance;
> in your book were written, every one of them,
> the days that were formed for me,
> when as yet there was none of them.
> How precious to me are your thoughts, O God! (v. 14b-17a)

What is our conclusion, when faced with all of this? Most basically, let us simply say this: **Mary invites us to take refuge in her maternal "womb," so that, in this intimate space, we may experience anew God's loving gaze, his healing and re-creating love, as he first created us in the womb of our natural mother.** This is the way in which, so deeply, Mary is and yearns to be our spiritual mother, in whose womb we are knitted together into a living and life-giving intimacy with God.

Reflection Questions:

— *When I open my nakedness to God's loving gaze, I find myself not only cherished by this gaze, but touched, healed, and transformed. Am I, however, afraid of encountering this gaze? Do I flee from the light of his eyes? Why?*

— *When I look into myself, can I see the two realities that I carry within me— the inheritance of sin and yet also the beauty of God's "fingerprint" in my unique identity? From which place do I habitually live? How can I live more deeply from the inner truth of God's love?*

DAY 25: TO SIMPLY LIVE IN LOVE

Each one of us bears within us an unspeakably profound and unrepeatably unique beauty—the unique image that God sees when he gazes upon us in love. Indeed, this image is constituted precisely by the Father's gaze, since for him *to look* is for him *to love*, and for him *to love* is for him *to bestow beauty and goodness*. When we allow ourselves to be led back to this place of vulnerable loving encounter, we come "home" to the authentic truth of our being as it ever flows as a pure gift from the hands and the Heart of God. In turn, the more we "get in touch" with this truth of our identity before God, the more that it can spread through the rest of our being to touch, to heal, and to transform us in the likeness of the One who calls us to intimacy with himself. This is how the love of God for us can gradually overcome the inheritance of sin that threatens to keep us away from him, that tempts us to close ourselves off from his gaze and from his invitation to intimacy.

It is true that no one else can pronounce for me my "Yes" to God's love. No one else can stand in my place and experience his loving gaze…since this gaze is directed uniquely at me alone, and it addresses my own freedom. On the other hand, on my own strength or initiative alone, I cannot adequately pronounce this "Yes." I find the obstacles within me too great. How then can I pronounce the "Yes" that I alone can give, if I, alone, cannot give it?

When Mary, in her own unique existence, experienced the loving gaze of God, she—because of the prevenient grace that had preserved her from the inheritance of original sin—was able to pronounce a complete and unreserved "Yes." She was able to open her heart entirely to welcome God's gift of love and to give herself totally in return. Further, as the New Eve she pronounced this "Yes," not only in her own name, but in the name of all humanity. In her consent to God's love and his invitation, she accepted the childlike dependency against which the first Eve had rebelled. In her "Yes," she opened herself to the fullness of the Father's love as his beloved daughter; she opened herself to the fullness of the Spirit's overshadowing presence in bridal receptivity, through which she conceived; she opened herself to the very incarnate presence of the Son, who became a man within her maternal womb.

As daughter, bride, and mother, Mary has allowed God to open up the space in which God's love finds full acceptance, and in which humanity can enter back into communion with God. She is like a "rose among thorns" (Sg 2:2), an immaculate virgin in the midst of a broken world; and in this purity she acts as a leaven in the dough of humanity, so that we too may share in her purity. Adam and Eve were the first in a long line of humanity subject to suffering and death, and knotted to the disorders of pride, possessiveness, and lust. And each of these three disordered movements—this "knot" of sinful desire which pulls our hearts from the center to the periphery, from unity to fragmentation—is an expression of the fundamental insecurity that we bear within us of feeling that we have lost God and his Love.

Let us then, in the next few reflections, delve more deeply into the nature of this "openness of heart" which allows God to restore us to the love and intimacy that was lost in sin—the openness which is directly contrary to the threefold movement of pride, possessiveness, and lust. We said that this openness of heart is precisely the single yet threefold reality of obedience, poverty, and chastity. Adam and Eve before sin bore these three dispositions within them as God's gift, and yet, when asked to confirm them through an act of trusting surrender to God, they instead chose to turn away. Let us try in some way to glimpse what the state before original sin would have been like. This will help us, then to see how it is radiantly restored (and more than restored) in the Virgin Mary and her beloved Son, Jesus Christ—who as the New Adam and the New Eve open the way for the healing and transformation of each one of us.

Adam and Eve, before sin, were **poor** because, like the little children that they were (spiritually speaking), they allowed the heavenly Father to care for them in his immense generosity. They remained with open hands and open heart to receive and to give at every moment, in a sensitivity that is the very opposite of possessiveness. Everything in their existence, from the creation that surrounded them to the very structure of their body and spirit, was welcomed as a pure and undeserved gift in radiant gratitude, and in gratitude it was placed back in the hands of the Giver. In childlike simplicity they felt no need to "grasp" or to protect anything as their "private possession," but rather welcomed without fear each instant of life in the depths of its beauty...a beauty that always surpasses anything human hands or heart can fully control or comprehend.

Their **obedience** flowered precisely from this attitude of childlike poverty, from this disposition of confident trust in the goodness and love of the Father. If they truly knew and believed in the love of God, if they understood and saw all as his gift, then all that was necessary for them was to live according to this gift. Their obedience was simply a way of allowing their lives to unfold in accord with the loving intentions of God which were inscribed into every fiber of creation and impressed upon their very being. Further, to live in this childlike trust, in this loving docility to God's ceaseless gift and guidance, was to find their hearts flowering in freedom. For obedience was not a burden, an arbitrary yoke, an external imposition forced on Adam and Eve from the outside. No, it was simply the space in which the gift of Love from the outside touched, enveloped, and brought to full flowering the deepest desires in the human heart.

Finally, they were **chaste** because their gaze was one of pure love, a gaze that was directed only to reverence, to cherish, and to affirm the other—and to welcome the loving gaze of the other in return. Indeed, this mutual gaze was but a reflection and an extension of the loving gaze of God himself, which each experienced casting its light forth in their inmost being and irradiating their entire life. They were naked without experiencing shame, because there was as yet no cause for fear or hesitation in beholding the nakedness and vulnerability of another, nor, on the other hand, in being seen. Shame comes only after original sin, because sin profoundly twists and corrupts the desires of the human heart and its spontaneous way of seeing and perceiving others.

Shame is a defense mechanism—and often a valid one—in which a person feels threatened by the look of another out of fear of being mistreated, abused, or used. On the other hand, shame can also be experienced in the one beholding, in that they become aware that their spontaneous reaction to seeing another is not a valid reaction of love, but a movement of lust or possessiveness. In this sense shame restrains the beholder from giving expression to the disordered movements of his or her fractured heart. Shame can also, however, be disordered, when it keeps the human heart from opening itself to another when trust is called for, when authentic love is truly encountered. Above all, shame is destructive when it causes us to flee from the face of God, to hide our guilt and brokenness from him in fear, rather than opening it to his healing gaze of mercy.

Before their consent to sin, the gaze of Adam and Eve was pure, and thus they were able to behold one another in reverence and love. When Adam gazed upon Eve, he saw shining from her entire physical being the unique beauty of her individual identity in the eyes of God...and he reverenced, loved, and sheltered this identity. The same is true for what Eve beheld in Adam. They knew that each person was a gift flowing unceasingly from the creative hands of God, and their first responsibility was to reverence this gift, to cradle it in the shelter of humble love. Only within this context of profound reverence were they also able to give expression to the mutual self-giving that would bind them together "in one flesh." Indeed, before original sin, the sexual union—if it even would have occurred in a way comparable to the way it is expressed in our fallen state—would have been in harmony with virginity, and not against it. Further, the bodily element of mutual self-giving would not have posed the danger of "submerging" the spirit in the flesh and of losing sight of the person. Rather, the body would simply have been the expression of the deeper and more intimate mystery: the joining of hearts and lives within the single, all-enveloping Love of God.

Reflection Questions:

— *When I reflect on poverty as simply the childlike attitude of trust in the Father's love, and the gratitude that feels no need to possess...how do I see this being expressed in my own life?*

— *When I reflect on obedience as receiving the Father's gift of love and living according to this gift in such a way that my freedom and happiness flower in precisely this way...how do I see this being expressed in my own life?*

— *When I reflect on chastity as the pure gaze of love that reverences and cherishes another, and also receives their gaze in trusting confidence, allowing a deepening intimacy to blossom between persons in mutual self-giving...how do I see this being expressed in my own life?*

DAY 26: BECAUSE YOU HOLD ME, I CAN OPEN MYSELF TO YOU

When we turn our gaze to our Virgin Mother, we immediately recognize that she beautifully incarnates the threefold disposition of poverty, obedience, and chastity about which we spoke in the previous reflection. Adam and Eve, before their sin, experienced this openness as a gift and a promise; but in them it never reached its full flowering in a perfect and enduring union with God. Rather, when they sinned, their hearts—open before in childlike trust to the Father and to each other—collapsed in on themselves in fear, in pride, possessiveness, and lust, enslaving them to fragmentation and superficiality. God fashioned Mary, however, as a New Eve, in a state of virginal and sinless openness which, throughout her life, would bring to full flower what had failed to be realized in our first parents. Yes, in her life—joined inseparably to the life of her Son, the New Adam—the wounds of sin would be healed. The state of pure love would be restored and, indeed, brought to a consummation that it had never reached before. Let us begin to see how this is so.

We already saw the radiance of this interior attitude of love in Mary during week two, when we spoke of the scene of the Annunciation. We saw how she, because of her certainty in being infinitely loved and cradled ceaselessly in the arms of Love, was able to open herself totally and without hesitation to welcome the gift and the invitation of God, and to abandon herself to him entirely in return. Her heart, in other words, was totally poor, obedient, and chaste in the simple "open-handedness" of a beloved child.

She was, and is, one of the "little ones" of Almighty God, whose very littleness magnifies his greatness—because this littleness does not close in on itself, it does not calculate, it does not place limits, but rather opens itself to the immensity of Love. It abandons its littleness into the Ocean of Love and Mercy, like a drop of water mingled together with the ever surging waves of the divine heartbeat, washing up unceasingly on the shores of creation and of every human heart. Indeed this trusting littleness is like that drop of water placed in the wine of the chalice at Mass, which then both together become the precious Blood of Jesus Christ. As the priest prays when he mingles the water and the wine: "May we share in the divinity of Christ, who humbled himself to share in our humanity." Mary gave this humanity which Jesus took to himself, and only through her was he able to receive as his own the humanity of all of us...which he then transformed into the Eucharist, the space of intimate encounter and union between God and humanity.

Her littleness, in other words, was not a closed resistance to God and his ineffable Love, but rather a complete openness to it. Her whole being was open in a **poverty** that was but an expression of love. It was indeed a reflection of the "divine poverty" lived by the three divine Persons in the bosom of the Trinity—where the Father, Son, and Holy Spirit are eternally open before one another without the least grasping or possessiveness. They are united, rather, in a ceaseless movement of mutual self-giving and reverent acceptance, which is so intimate and so total that they live together a single life of love, abiding within one another in an unspeakable mutual indwelling. In poverty Mary let herself be held, in faith, in the depths of this divine embrace. And in the concrete circumstances of her life, she let herself be cared for unceasingly by this God who alone can provide for his children the necessities of their life, whether physical or spiritual. Her whole life exhibited, in other words, the truth of that pronouncement of her Son: "Do not be anxious, for your Father knows..."

Her **obedience**, too, was but an expression of love—and of her complete trust in God and his goodness—in which she welcomed all that came from him at every moment, and lived according to his gift. Indeed, she allowed herself to be taken by the hand and led where she herself could not go on her own, and where, indeed, she did not know or foresee the way. But as long as the Beloved was there calling her, that was enough—for his word, his invitation, his Love was all that was necessary. Indeed, her obedience was an active and generous responsiveness to the Love that she had first received, and continued to receive unceasingly at every instant. It was an expression of her yearning to offer her life as a "home" for the love and the presence of God; her yearning to correspond, in love, with his own loving intentions; and, finally, her yearning to enter into ever deeper intimacy with the Beloved in whose embrace alone was her true and lasting rest.

This, clearly, has brought us to the meaning of her **chastity** and virginity, which is but a flower and fruit of the reality of her poverty and obedience. It is the manifestation of her total belonging to God, in which she becomes both spouse and mother. Her whole being, body and spirit, is placed in his divine hands, in the ardent thirst for an ever deeper intimacy with him and also in the thirst to allow him to pour forth, in her and through her, the depths of his healing and transforming Love. Her chastity allows her life to be completely transparent to the radiance of the Light of Divine Love, and indeed allows her to see, to know, and to love within the beauty of this Light—to be God's beloved, and to love unceasingly from within this Love.

In a sense we can say that poverty, obedience, and chastity are the space in which Mary's littleness allows itself to be espoused to God's Immensity. And this is true for each one of us. When we allow God to touch and open our hearts through his Love, we can find our littleness joined to his greatness, sheltered in the Ocean of Mercy and infinite Tenderness. Yes, in this way God opens our heart to freely consent to being cradled in the all-enveloping arms of his Love. In this way he opens us to allow his Love to irradiate the whole of our being and existence, and to manifest himself freely within it. Precisely in this encounter and union between littleness and Immensity, tininess and Infinity, the human heart finds peace and joy—for we were created precisely for this purpose: **to rest in the arms of a Love so great, so pure, so perfect, that nothing can overcome it, and yet a Love so tender, so intimate, so close, that it sees us, knows us, and embraces us at every moment and throughout everything.**

Reflection Questions:

— Do I see how Mary's openness in love was but an expression of the Love that she had first received? How she was able to confidently receive and give because of her trust in the undying goodness of God?

— When I reflect on what is said above about poverty, obedience, and chastity, what particularly stands out to me? What do I find my heart desiring? What may I perhaps struggle with?

DAY 27: SURRENDERED TO THE MYSTERY

The statements we have already made about Mary are deeply rooted in Scripture, in the specific reality that unveils itself before our eyes in what the Word of God says about the Virgin Mother. But let us make this more explicit by immersing ourselves in Scripture directly. Let us, by looking at the concrete unfolding of Mary's life, try to go deeper into her inner disposition, to draw near to her heart.

The Gospels are clear that Mary knows and experiences her littleness and her limitations—her complete dependence upon God—but they are also clear that she is touched, enfolded, and sustained by grace, by the loving kindness of God. She speaks explicitly about this encounter between littleness and greatness in her *Magnificat*: "He has regarded the lowliness of his handmaid...and he who is mighty has done great things for me, and holy is his name. He has exalted those of low degree; he has filled the hungry with good things" (cf. Lk 1:48-53).

During the event of the Annunciation Mary manifests such humility, such lighthearted unselfconsciousness, that she does not fret about her smallness in a way that would hinder the activity of grace. Rather, she lays bare her soul and body to welcome the gift that God desires to give...the very incarnation of the divinity within the confines of her womb, who clothes himself with flesh through her flesh. That God has asked is enough for her—that he has spoken and asked for her permission is enough to awaken her "Yes." She trusts that he will take care of the rest, as the angel himself assures her: "With God nothing is impossible" (Lk 1:37). And she is blessed because she believes in God's word, even without seeing, as Elizabeth exclaims to her: "Blessed is she who believed that there would be a fulfillment of what was spoken to her from the Lord" (Lk 1:45). This makes us think of the words of Jesus at the end of John's Gospel, which apply to Mary in a special way: "Blessed are those who have not seen and yet believe" (Jn 20:29).

Further, Mary's openness to the divine Mystery continually deepens and matures throughout her life, as God leads her on a "pilgrimage of faith," in which her own existence is plunged more and more into the abyss of God's presence and activity incarnate in her Son, Jesus Christ.

The whole of her life is just a reaffirmation and an unfolding of the words she spoke in response to God's love addressing her through the angel Gabriel: "Let it be to me according to your word" (Lk 1:38). There are many times when she "does not see," when she does not understand, but she nonetheless clings in radical trust to the goodness and love of God. Or more accurately, she allows herself to be held by the Love that has cradled her from her earliest days, and which she trusts will never abandon her. This trust, this innermost attitude of restfulness in the enfolding Love of God, allows her to walk, step by step, along the path that God gradually marks out for her.

When she brings the child Jesus to the temple shortly after his birth, presenting him according to the law, she hears that mysterious prophecy of Simeon:

> Behold, this child is set for the fall
> and rising of many in Israel,
> and he will be a sign of contradiction
> —and indeed a sword will pierce your own soul also—
> that the thoughts out of many hearts may be revealed.
> (Lk 2:34-35)

Jesus comes as the Light of the world, in order to bring forth from the darkness all who are willing to open their hearts to him. And yet this Light also evokes the forces of darkness which hate and resist the Light:

> God so loved the world that he gave his only-begotten Son, that whoever believes in him should not perish but have eternal life. ... And this is the judgment, that the light has come into the world, and men loved darkness rather than light, because their deeds were evil. For every one who does evil hates the light, and does not come to the light, lest his deeds should be exposed. But he who does what is true comes to the light, that it may be clearly seen that his deeds have been wrought in God. (John 3:16, 19-21)

Mary will be caught up into this encounter between Light and darkness, into this movement by which God's infinite Compassion descends into our anguish and suffering, there to take us up into itself, to consume our misery in the fires of Mercy, and to carry us back into the divine embrace. She will be there as one whose heart and life is totally and unreservedly open to the Light, who welcomes it entirely and lets herself be bathed in its radiance—even in the darkest of places.

We don't know how much of this she understood, how much she was able to grasp the meaning and mystery of the Passion and Resurrection of Jesus. But we have ample evidence that her life unfolded in an ever deepening surrender, in a trust that allowed her to abandon herself ever anew to God's loving invitation. And this trusting abandonment, we believe, also opened the way for a true understanding, which, in matters such as these, is but the resonance of the heart before the activity of Love made present in every moment and circumstance.

When Jesus stayed behind in the temple at the age of twelve, and Mary and Joseph looked for him in anguish, finally finding him after three days, Mary asked him, "Son, why have you done this to us?" He simply replied: "Why do you look for me? Did you not know that I must be in the house of my Father?" The Gospel explicitly says that "they did not understand what he said to them," but notes that "Mary kept all these things in her heart" (cf. Lk 2:41-51). In other words, Mary is brought face to face with an event whose full meaning she cannot understand. In this way she is invited to reflect, to pray, to contemplate, in order to enter more deeply into the unspeakable mystery of Jesus in his intimacy with the Father—not, as she had known it before, in the tenderness of an infant and a child under her care—but as the sovereign freedom of Love that surpasses all human bonds while cradling them, and the whole of creation, within its tender embrace. This embrace is a Tenderness which, while surpassing her expectations or previous experiences of tender human love, is not less, but more profound and more true.

And Mary consents to enter into this "unknowing," with a faith that goes beyond the limitations of human understanding, beyond the narrowness of the human wish to be in control. However, her faith is not therefore "blind," in the sense that it has no motives, nor that it does not care to seek for vision. Rather, her faith—her radical and unhesitating trust and surrender to God's plan—is but a response to God's grace and love, and allows God to lead her ever deeper into authentic understanding. Blessed indeed are those who, without having seen, believe. And yet their very faith opens their eyes and their hearts to see, to receive illumination, and to enter into a profound intimacy with the Mystery of the One who unceasingly desires to communicate himself.

Reflection Questions:

— How is it that littleness, while remaining little, can nonetheless allow itself to be opened to the Immensity of God's Mystery which surpasses all comprehension and experience, and yet cradles us ceaselessly within itself?

— Mary walks a "pilgrimage of faith," placing her trust entirely in God and his Love—such that her faith, her hope, and her love are the very foundation of her whole life. It is precisely this (living in faith, hope, and love) which allows her to be immersed into ever deeper union with God. In what way is my life founded on faith, hope, and love? Or in what way may God be inviting me to a more total surrender?

DAY 28: THE VICTORY OF ETERNAL LOVE

We spoke about how Mary's faith, hope, and love—her trusting surrender to God in poverty, obedience, and chastity—allows God to lead her ever deeper into the depths of his Love. This "pilgrimage of faith" climaxes in the Passion of Jesus and finds its confirmation and consummation in his Resurrection. Mary's radical trust in the Father, and in his Son who so powerfully enters into and transforms her life, allows her to follow Jesus even to the foot of his Cross. She does this, as we have said, not by breaking down the boundaries of her littleness, her human limitations, her dependency, but simply by allowing herself to be cradled and carried by Eternal Love at every moment. This Love communicates itself to her in and through the very concrete reality of each moment, through which it swathes her entire existence like a seamless fabric.

Let us turn back to Scripture and see the path Mary walks toward the fullness of the Paschal Mystery. Let us try to see how Jesus begins to draw Mary from the intimacy that she knew with him in his youth to a union more mysterious and yet more intimate—at the heart of the Cross and Resurrection. This process, as we saw yesterday, begins already in his infancy with the prophecy of Simeon, and in his adolescence with his staying three days in the temple (a clear prophecy of the "loss" of Christ during the three days between his death and his Resurrection).

Further, during his public ministry Jesus explicitly prepares Mary for the new and deeper form of relationship to which he is inviting her. He shifts the very locus of their relationship from the flesh to the spirit—from a natural human intimacy to an ineffable divine communion. Of course, this spiritual union was the core of Mary's relationship with Christ from the beginning, but now he is leading her out, through a kind of "night of faith," into a yet more profound and total reliance on absolute Love. **This Love is the space in which their relationship can be sustained, and in which it can also flower in ever deeper communion.**

In other words, Mary is drawn to an ever deepening reliance upon the Love that cradles her life entirely within itself—a Love that provides security and stability, not merely in times of palpable consolation, but also in times of struggle and darkness. By living in faith Mary opens her being to welcome the Light that shines brilliantly even in difficult moments—finding herself drawn closer to Christ and to the Father even, and perhaps especially, in these places. In this way, her relationship with her Son—and with the entire Trinity—is continually deepened. On the other hand, this deepening itself is sustained at every moment within the already present Love which cradles her unceasingly.

When, during his ministry, Jesus is told about Mary's presence —"Your mother and your brethren are seeking for you"—Jesus speaks about the new bonds of love which create a family that surpasses the bonds of flesh: "Whoever does the will of my Father is my brother, my sister, and my mother" (cf. Mk 3:32-35). Jesus has come into a human family and made its life his own, but he has done so, ultimately, in order to create in himself a new and universal family, a family sharing in the very life of the Family of the Trinity. He therefore directs the attention of all to the absolute Love—the "will of my Father"—which he desires to be the very "space" in which all hearts can be truly and eternally united.

At another time, when his mother is praised—"Blessed is the womb that bore you and the breasts that nursed you"—Jesus replies: "Blessed rather are those who hear the word of God and keep it" (cf. Lk 11:27-28). Surely Mary heard the word of God and kept it! We have seen this very clearly. She is blessed, not because of a mere physical union with Christ, but because, as Elizabeth said: "Blessed is she who believed that what was spoken to her from the Lord would be fulfilled" (Lk 1:45). True blessedness cannot be reduced to a physical relationship, to the merely human sphere. Rather, all human love is invited to open itself to the horizons of infinite Love, received in faith and obedience, in the poverty of a trusting and virginal heart.

Mary, too, had to undergo this path of deepening and transformation, not because of any sin or impurity in her love, but simply because of the very nature of love itself. God invited her to walk the path by which this world becomes ever more transparent to the eternal Mystery, by which the veil of mortality is stretched thin to allow the light of Eternity to shine through. It is only within this Love, within this all-enfolding Mystery, that true and abiding blessedness can be found—and in which the goodness of the world can reveal its true meaning. This is, we might add, precisely the meaning of the Beatitudes (cf. Mt 5:1-12), in which the poor heart which relates to God and to others in vulnerable nakedness, in loving trust, is the one which is truly happy and blessed.

Throughout all of this, Mary clings to Christ—and clings, with Christ, to the loving and provident hand of the Father. She allows herself to enter, with him and in him, ever deeper into the sphere of the Trinity's Love. She finds the horizons of Love unfolding before her loving and contemplative gaze—surpassing her comprehension and yet enfolding her on every side. She enters, too, within this Love, into the Trinity's loving plan for the salvation of the world, into his intention to redeem all persons and unite them as one through the saving Passion and Resurrection of Jesus. This movement, which occurs throughout Jesus' life, therefore climaxes at the foot of the Cross and finds resolution on Easter morning. Jesus came in littleness and humility, living our life in the midst of this creation—as we ourselves experience it. But his ultimate desire was to take up our existence—our whole being and our whole life, in all of its joy and all of its anguish—into his own Compassionate Heart, in order to immerse it into the endless stream of the Trinity's life of love. This is what is accomplished through the Paschal Mystery, through Jesus' Eucharist, Passion, Resurrection, and Ascension.

And Mary, before everyone and in the name of everyone, allows herself to be inserted into the heart of this Mystery. She lets herself be led and carried, by the Love which has cradled her from the first moment of her existence, into the space of Christ' redeeming Passion. Here she is enfolded in the very mutual self-giving of the Father, Son, and Holy Spirit, in their ceaseless dialogue of love, which has now penetrated into the deepest darkness of the world in order to illuminate it from within. In this place of unspeakable suffering, in which she feels that she is losing her Son on the human level, something mysterious happens. **In this very place she is united with him yet more intimately, more deeply than she has ever been before…within the all-enveloping Mystery of Love which penetrates and transforms all.**

At the foot of the Cross, Mary's openness meets the openness of the Crucified One, who is naked, with his arms stretched wide, and indeed with his very Heart soon to be opened by a lance. And this mutual openness flowers in a shared self-giving, in which her "Yes" mingles together with his "Yes," and they both surge back in response to the perfect "Yes" of the Father. Her loving trust in God—her openness of heart in faith, hope, and love—has allowed God to lead her into the space of most intimate spousal union with himself...and to immerse her in the very Ocean of the Trinity's life.

She stands in this place, the Mother of Christ but also, through the profound mutual self-giving that occurs here, his Bride. Through her receptivity to the loving gift of Jesus, she allows Divine Love, which has knit their hearts together from the beginning, to show itself stronger than suffering and death. Yes, the bond of love that binds her heart to the Heart of her Son cannot be torn asunder. And this bond that joins them together is so strong, so pure, simply because it is an expression of the bond of that Eternal Love which cradles both of them unceasingly within itself: the enveloping Mystery of the Trinity's life.

Yes, in the place of suffering, in which Christ takes us into himself with the burden of our sin, our sorrow, and our unspeakable loneliness, he shows that Love is stronger than everything. He reveals that even in this place the Father gently cradles his beloved Son, holding him unceasingly in his undying Love. And therefore the Son, too, can hold and cradle us, pressing us to his loving Heart and carrying us, beyond the boundary of death, beyond our fears, our hesitations, our sins, into the fullness of the endless life of intimacy in the bosom of the Father, Son, and Holy Spirit.

Reflection Questions:

— It is precisely the "already" of God's cradling Love which enables Mary to let herself to be drawn into the "not yet" of ever deeper intimacy with Christ. In my own times of suffering, or in times when I feel myself invited to let go of control and trust more radically in God, am I able to rest in the "already" and the "always" of God's Love which holds and shelters me?

— Do I see how all natural human relationships, as good as they are, ultimately find their enduring meaning through their openness to the Eternal Love that wants to be expressed within them? And in the spiritual union toward which they are ordered, a union of hearts that, because it is rooted in God, continues into eternity and indeed finds its consummation there?

– *Am I able to see the union effected at the foot of the Cross, the self-giving of Mary and Jesus that flowers in a profound intimacy stronger even than death? Do I realize that I, too, am invited to experience this kind of unbreakable intimacy, precisely through the same kind of openness in total mutual self-giving?*

CONCLUDING DAYS

DAY 29: TRANSPARENT TO HIS LIGHT

We have come to the final days of reflection and preparation, and when we cast our glance back on the previous four weeks, we see that we have covered a great deal of ground. Or, better, we have gazed deeply and in a prolonged contemplation on the mystery of God's infinite and eternal Love as it cradles our world in itself, as it seeks to communicate itself to us and to find a home within our hearts, and to draw us to make our Home, in turn, in the bosom of the Trinity. We have seen how the Virgin Mary, being the first person to receive the gift of God in Christ—allowing the very incarnate flesh of the divine Son to be formed within her womb—is a kind of "meeting-place" between God and ourselves.

She is, as Saint Irenaeus said, the "cause of our salvation." In other words, because of her "Yes" to God's invitation, the eternal Son of the Father was able to come into our world and to redeem us through his complete loving gift of himself. God made his saving activity in this world, as it were, dependent upon the "Yes" of his creature, on the permission she would freely give to him. He must seek permission because he is all Love, because he is infinite Tenderness, which cannot force, cannot impose, but must first elicit a free response on the part of the beloved before he pours himself out into her. However, on the other hand, he also knows that, being a creature, she cannot even begin to say "Yes" unless he bestows upon her the ability...unless his grace goes before, awakens, and sustains her loving and trust-filled response.

Mary is the woman who, before all others, was cradled and sustained by God's grace in this way; she was and is "full of grace," bearing the fullness of God's very Being which holds and fills her. And this is because her consent to his Love is not hindered or obscured by the least shadow of sin—though, in turn, her freedom from sin, which allows her to speak such a consent, is itself God's gracious gift! Therefore all is, in the end, grace: Mary's "Yes" and her very ability to say "Yes," and yet such grace does not hinder, but makes possible, her freedom as a creature. And she is truly free to consent to him, free in love and by love—a love that heals the wound of Adam and Eve, who precisely in the name of "freedom" enslaved themselves to disobedience. Their supposed "autonomy" did not liberate them to follow their own way, but rather un-tethered them from the grace in which alone they could live and love truly and freely. Through untying this knot of sinful disobedience, by un-tethering our hearts from the slavery to sin that binds us, Mary opens us to be re-tethered to the loving will of God and his sustaining grace, in which alone we will find the full flowering of freedom in love.

Mary was and is, therefore, nothing but "Yes," with no hint of a "no" within her. Or rather, her total "Yes" to God is spontaneously a "no" to anything that would turn her away from God. But this no is not a violent renunciation or a rejection caused by fear, but a simple expression of the fact that her heart already belongs wholly to Another, and need not seek for anything outside of him. So full of the Trinity is she that nothing else has any room in her unless is belongs to him and bears his presence within it. Nonetheless, this very complete belonging to God, which makes no space within her for sin, allows her to see, to know, and to love all the works of God's hands in the true and authentic beauty. It allows her to gaze upon each one of us within the radiance of God's own loving gaze, loving us as he loves us.

Indeed, her very purity allows her, free from all sin, to welcome in compassion the burdens that we bear because of sin, and to hold them —to hold us—lovingly before the face of the Father. As Georges Bernanos so beautifully wrote in his novel, *The Diary of a Country Priest*:

> The eyes of Our Lady are the only real child-eyes that have ever been raised to our shame and sorrow. … they are not indulgent— for there is no indulgence without something of bitter experience —they are eyes of gentle pity, wondering sadness, and with something more in them, never yet known or expressed, something that makes her younger than sin, younger than the race from which she sprang, and though a mother, by grace, Mother of all graces, our little youngest sister.

In being the littlest child of God, she is truly the "Mother of all the living," truly the New Eve who sees sin for what it is and chooses instead the Tree of Life. Yes, she stands at the foot of this Tree, compassionately united with her Son and with each one of us…sharing in the work of healing and reconciliation that occurs here, within the Heart of

Jesus. In other words, she enters into the space of perfect Love—the meeting-place of the Sacred Heart of Jesus—and receives his gift and gives herself totally to him in return. United to God through this intimate self-giving, she is united also to each one of her brothers and sisters: as "the scattered children of God are gathered together into unity" in the Heart of the One who, "lifted up from the earth, draws all to himself" and reconciles us with the Trinity and with one another in the depths of his own tender Love (cf. Jn 11:52; 12:32).

Mary is like a transparent and pure pane of glass, through which divine Light freely passes into our world, not obstructed by the least impurity of grasping or possessiveness. She is the prism that receives the full and undivided outpouring of the Trinity's radiance and lets it refract forth into the world through her. She is so illumined by this Light that she appears, herself to be "all light," radiant in the gift that God has bestowed upon her. And yet such a privilege is not exclusive, since God has touched her in this way, not only because he loves her—which he does!—but because he also loves us, and wants us to contemplate in her the awesome things he desires to do in us as well. Yes, he wants us to share in the very dispositions of her heart, her loving and trust-filled openness, so that he can draw us, too, into the most intimate depths of his embrace.

Reflection Questions:

— *Mary's freedom consists precisely in her total, loving, and trust-filled "Yes" to God and his Love. And, through her, God desires to touch us, liberating us from the shackles of our fear and sin, so that we too can pronounce the same childlike "Yes." This is the meaning of Marian entrustment: to insert my "Yes" into her "Yes," so that she can perfect and sustain it. Am I ready and willing to do this?*

— *Do I understand how Mary's purity, her being "younger than sin," allows her to have a true and understanding compassion for every human heart? Do I realize that the same can be true for me—the more I belong to God, the more I can belong to my brothers and sisters in love?*

DAY 30: SHELTERED WITHIN HER "YES"

God invites us to be, as Mary is, a pure "Yes" to God, a "Yes" which is awakened and sustained by his own all-enveloping Love. This "Yes," before being an act of self-*giving*, is a simple willingness to *receive*, to welcome the outpouring love of God and the tenderness of his gaze. Indeed, this consent to receive is, in the last analysis, the deepest way to give oneself. It is our return into the interior sanctuary where we are alone before God, where we are intimately united to him in that space where he ceaselessly communicates himself to us, and, in himself, gives us the truth of our own personal being as his beloved child.

Through the outpouring of his grace, through the docility by which we allow his Love to touch us, to enfold us, and to possess us, our "Yes" can grow ever more total—so total that there is no room in us for the slightest turning away from God or from intimate communion with him. This is not a matter of no longer experiencing human frailty, but of letting our frailty be cradled always in the arms of his Love, which is our protection and our strength. Perhaps in this mortal life such a perfect "Yes" can only be approximated, since there always exists the possibility of our turning away, of our losing sight of God's love and his call. But just like a little child who can barely walk, as long as she does not refuse to allow herself to be upheld by her parents, no fall will ever separate her from their enveloping arms. They will protect and hold her, in her frailty, in the shelter of their love. How much more can God can sustain us throughout this life, like a parent their child, carrying us toward the fullness that awaits us at the end of time. In heaven, our freedom will reach its full flowering in the perfect security of God's Love, which upholds and consummates our own loving "Yes"...a "Yes" to his Love which can nevermore be revoked or lessened in any way.

The "Yes" that awaits us then, when we at last see God face to face, will be a "Yes" that corresponds perfectly with the "Yes" which God himself pronounces in the inmost depths of our being—his ineffable Love by which he cries out: "You are my beloved child, in whom I delight!" Our response will simply be an eternal cry of reciprocal jubilation and total surrender: "And you, my God, are my loving Father, my Beloved, my Life, my Joy! I surrender myself to you without reserve, because I trust in you, because I know your Love, and because I am drawn by your Beauty... In you alone can I rest...while in turn, Beloved, I give you permission to make your home, your place of repose, in my heart."

God has intended, in choosing Mary to become his Mother, that we may all share in the mystery first lived by her. He has intended that her "Yes" become the space in which the "Yes" of every human heart finds security and strength—even in the fragility and uncertainty of this life. But this is simply because her "Yes" is inseparably united to the perfect "Yes" of the eternal Son. As Pope Benedict XVI has said:

> The "yes" of the Son: "I have come to do your will," and the "yes" of Mary: "Let it be to me according to your word"—this double "yes" becomes a single "yes," and thus the Word becomes flesh in Mary. In this double "yes" the obedience of the Son is embodied, and by her own "yes" Mary gives him that body. "Woman, what have I to do with you?" Ultimately, what each has to do with the other is found in this double "yes" which resulted in the Incarnation. The Lord's answer [to his Mother at Cana] points to this point of profound unity. It is precisely to this that he points his Mother. Here, in their common "yes" to the will of the Father, an answer is found. We too need to learn always anew how to progress towards this point; there we will find the answer to our questions. (9-11-06, Altötting, Bavaria)

This "point" of profound unity—in which our "Yes" is melded together as one with the single "Yes" of Mary and Jesus to the Father—this is the point in which we find the security that we thirst for so much. We can be moved to fear and anxiety when we turn our gaze to our own inconstancy, to the struggles we have in keeping our heart always open for God's Love, to the disordered movements within us. But the essential truth is that **our whole existence is already cradled within the perfect "Yes" of God, who has created us out of love and for love. However much we falter and feel our inadequacy, our inadequacy is nonetheless sustained by the perfect Love of God and his wholehearted "Yes" to us.** He is the God of everlasting fidelity, the God who cannot go back on his promises, the God who has entrusted himself entirely to us. And this very divine entrustment awakens, and can sustain until the end, our own loving entrustment in return. As long as we desire to say this "Yes," as long as we never cease trying to entrust ourselves to God, he can and will take care of the rest.

Mary shows us that this is possible. It is possible for God, and it is possible for the real human heart within the limits and struggles of this world. She shows the true beauty of the human heart, the real possibility offered to every one of us. In her consent to God, in her fidelity to him, in her "Yes" that was always sheltered in his Love, she reveals the true and deepest vocation of every person. In this "Yes" she allowed God to truly be her Father, to draw near and to unite her to himself in intimate love, and to become present in this world in a unique way in and through her.

Further, this "Yes" transformed and gave meaning to each moment of her life, allowing her to recognize and receive his Love unceasingly in all things. In this "Yes," God held and sustained her even through the anguish of the Cross; he held her in the arms of the Love that was stronger than suffering and death. In this "Yes" she joyfully welcomed the Risen Jesus as he came to her, radiant with the glory of eternal Love which had now poured itself into our world in the most radical and total way. In this "Yes" she welcomed the Holy Spirit who descended on the Church at Pentecost, bringing forth spiritually the fullness of the mystical Body of Christ, just as Mary had brought forth his earthly body so many years ago at Christmas. Finally, because of this "Yes," which echoed ceaselessly from the very loving "Yes" of God, Mary was unable to be separated from the fullness of Life even by the ending of her mortal existence. The one who belongs totally to Life cannot experience enduring death. Therefore, Mary allowed God, who had always held her in his Love from the first moment of her conception, to hold her still, taking her, body and soul—in the whole of her being—into the bosom of his own Trinitarian embrace.

To entrust oneself into the loving hands and heart of Mary is simply to place our frail and fragile "Yes" within the sheltering "Yes" of our heavenly Mother. It is to join our "Yes," in and through her, with the perfect "Yes" of Jesus Christ to his heavenly Father. It is, above all, to recognize and to consent to the cradling arms of God's Love, which enfold and shelter us at every moment. It is, as it were, simply giving

God our consent to his Love:

"Yes, my God, I give you permission to hold me as you desire—to hold me, shelter me, and sustain me as you did Mary! She is already with you in the fullness of heavenly glory; she is already in that place where her whole being is forevermore a pure 'Yes' to you, cradled in your own perfect loving 'Yes.' I want to be there too, and, in faith, I am already given a foretaste of this intimacy. So hold me, my God, hold me in your Love which is stronger than all, and carry me at last into that place where I so deeply desire to be...and where you desire me to be even more."

Reflection Questions:

– Do I feel that, nearing the end of these weeks, I am ready to offer my consent to God, and to Mary, in a deeper and more total way that I have before?

– What most do I desire this "Yes" to bring about in my life? In other words, what areas of my life need most especially to be placed within the cradling arms of God's Love, there to receive his transforming touch and the security of his embrace?

DAY 31: TO FEEL WITH THE HEART OF THE CHURCH

There are two beautiful Latin phrases that, in the light of our previous reflections, reveal their profound beauty and radiance. The first phrase is: *sentire cum Ecclesia*. This means "to think with the Church," or, more accurately, "to feel with the Church," "to share in the very sentiments of the Church." The other phrase, which expresses much the same meaning, is used to express a life that authentically flows from a "Catholic" vision, a vision irradiated by the Mystery of God's Love shining in the heart of his Church: *ex corde Ecclesiae*. "From the heart of the Church." We can combine these two phrases to express the inner truth of holiness of which we have been speaking: *sentire cum corde Ecclesiae*—to feel with the very heart of the Church. **What we have been trying to do throughout these weeks of reflection is precisely to experience the pulsing heartbeat that surges unceasingly in the heart of the Church...and to feel it as an intimate motherly heart, indeed as a heart which simply echoes with the reverberations of the heart of the Trinity who lives within her.**

We have seen—hopefully we have even felt—that this heartbeat is not the heartbeat of a mere "institution," nor even of a mere society or community on the model of every other political or social body in this world. No, the Church is an intimate family, a communion of brothers and sisters bound together by the single thread of the ineffable Love of God. Everything within the Church—all of her institutions and laws, the priestly ministry entrusted to the successors of the Apostles, the radiant beauty of her sacramental life, the breathtaking harmony and depth of her teaching and doctrine—**all of this flows from, returns to, and serves this mystery of loving intimacy with God and with our brothers and sisters.** Nowhere, therefore, can we better discern the contours of this inner mystery of the Church, nowhere can we better feel her heartbeat, than in drawing near to our Blessed Mother, the Virgin Mary. For she has lived this all before us, and she has lived it also for our sake.

Mary bears the whole Church in her fullness within her own maternal bosom, even before the Church is fully born from the wounded side of Christ as he hangs upon the Cross, just as Eve was born from the side of Adam. Mary is there at the foot of the Cross, the Tree of Life, as the woman who—in the name of the Church and of all her children throughout the centuries—receives the outpouring gift of the Bridegroom's Love. She is there, united to Christ in an unspeakably deep and enduring intimacy, which no suffering, no pain, and not even death can tear asunder. Therefore she is also there, vigilant in faith, hope, and love, when Jesus rises on Easter morning; and she welcomes him with a receptive, trusting, and virginal heart. Finally, now that her Son has ascended to the right hand of the Father and has sent the Spirit into the world—and she has joined him there in the bosom of the Trinity—Mary continues to be present in the heart of the Church, unceasingly at work in the life of each one of us. She simply cooperates with the work of the Blessed Trinity in this world, seeking to be the sheltering "womb" in which God continually loves us, touches us, and prepares us for the final rebirth at the end of our life.

The ancient Christian writer, Origen, called a person who lives this heartbeat of the Church—in other words, the inner "Marian mystery" that illumines the whole life of the Church—an "ecclesial soul." An *ecclesial soul* is a person who, in their very individuality—in the very depths of their unique and unrepeatable intimacy with God—allows their heart to expand to share in the very mystery of the universal Church as she tenderly embraces humanity. Their own personal life, while not being destroyed or absorbed, is opened wide to a greater mystery and participates in it—indeed, they find themselves truly precisely by receiving the gift that can only come from the outside. This Mystery, first of all, is simply God himself, who gently cradles his precious child, his beloved spouse, within his embrace, and gives them the ineffable joy of knowing and experiencing his Love. As we saw in our reflections on the child in the arms of her mother, to be open to the great mystery of Love, to be utterly surrendered to the Immensity of the One transcends us and yet intimately holds us, is not to lose ourselves, but to find ourselves truly...cradled in the arms of perfect Love.

Within the bosom of the Trinity, from the heart of the intimate and unique encounter that we have with him, our hearts can truly allow themselves to be opened, totally and unconditionally, to love as he loves, embracing every person within the world in a vulnerable and tender receptivity. This is the great gift that comes to us through our incorporation into the Church, through our adoption into the family of God and into the very life of the Holy Trinity. We find our individuality, which has become narrowed and collapsed in upon itself in sin, re-opened radically to the enveloping Love of the Father, Son, and Holy Spirit. And in our communion with him, in our entrance into the "new world" of grace and love, we discover anew every person whom God has made, radiant in the light of his own loving gaze.

This openness to the immense Mystery of God, and to the bonds of intimacy that he knits together throughout the universe in his own Love, was realized first and most deeply in the Virgin Mary. Her heart was totally open to this expansiveness, as we have seen, in such a way that she truly became the "ecclesial soul" par excellence—in a way the very "Church-in-person"—in her unspeakably intimate union with the Trinity, and her union with every person from within the bosom of the Trinity.

In her the *personal* and the *communal* are not in opposition, but find a profound harmony—simply because she lives all from love and for love, belonging entirely to the One who made her. She is one who, through living totally in relationship with God—in complete dependence upon him at every moment—experiences the joy of being held unceasingly by Another, of living her own personal existence, not isolated within herself, but as a ceaseless relationship of love. Indeed, through this constant and all-enveloping relationship with God, she is a woman whose entire personality is utterly open to the community—to the community of the Father, Son, and Holy Spirit, and to the community of the Church that would be formed through sharing in the life of the Trinity. In other words, through her surrender into the abyss of the Trinity's Love, she allowed her heart to be dilated to embrace the entire world, and to carry us all within herself…as she herself is held within the embrace of God.

Each one of us is invited to share in this "*sentire cum corde Ecclesiae*," to let our lives be immersed in the mystery of the Church, in the mystery of intimacy that God yearns to establish with all of humanity. In this way, indeed, we will see how our lives are gradually healed from the wounds of fear and sin and re-opened to the relationships that give life and joy. Through letting God draw us to himself—in and through the embrace of our Mother, the Church—we can find ourselves cradled in the arms of perfect Love once again. Yes, we can find our hearts expanding boundlessly into communion with the Trinity and with every person. Thus we can know the fullness of the Reality that, as a child, we only glimpsed, truly but imperfectly, in the smile of our mother.

Reflection Questions:

— Do I feel in myself a desire for, or a sharing in, this "inner heartbeat of the Church," which is intimate communion with God and with others within the Love of God?

— Do I see how Mary reveals, and safeguards, the intimate personal character of the Church, so that the Church never becomes an "impersonal institution"? In other words, do I see how Mary reveals the tender maternal (and spousal) heart of the Church, in which each individual is seen, loved, and desired absolutely and uniquely?

DAY 32: TYING IT ALL TOGETHER

Let us offer a summary of some central themes from our journey over these last weeks. Obviously, we cannot express everything, because the richness of the mysteries that we have been contemplating surpasses our comprehension (and therefore even more any comprehensive summary!). But we will recall some of the most important points, in order to tie our reflections together and, especially, to prepare us (tomorrow) to formulate a personal prayer of entrustment to Mary, which truly expresses the dispositions of our heart.

In week 1 we looked at the "foundational experience" of love that lies at the origin of the life of each one of us: the experience of being loved by another, of receiving myself as a gift from another in such a way that I remain always cradled within the enveloping arms of their love. We saw how the relationship between mother and child is a kind of "sanctuary" that God has preserved in the midst of creation in order to express this love and to bestow this experience, which then paves the way for all future experiences of life. When all is seen as coming from love and returning to love, as enfolded always in love, then we can live in childlike playfulness and joy, in a trusting self-surrender that feels no need to protect or isolate oneself from others or from the world around us. Such loving and trust-filled openness, we said, is a very reflection of the openness of the Father, Son, and Holy Spirit in their endless life of intimacy.

However, we were also led to speak about the "rupture" that has been caused by sin, precisely in the seamless fabric of love and intimacy. Through our own personal sin, as well as the wounds afflicted on us by others or by the circumstances of life, we can be pulled away from the Love that has created us and always sustains us. Though God is ever close, ever enfolding us, our hearts can become closed in upon themselves in fear, in shame, in disordered grasping. This is why Christ became man—entered into our own "foundational experience" of love in the arms of Mary, his mother—and espoused our humanity to himself. Indeed, he descended even into our experience of anguish and isolation, yet not to be overcome by the darkness, but to overcome the darkness with the Light. He is perfect Love descending into our narrow places of lovelessness, in order to break all open from within by the expansiveness of his own self-giving. Yes, he crosses over the rift that has been opened between us and God—the lack of intimate loving relationship for which we were made—and, within the sinews of his own Sacred Heart, weaves us back together again, in a seamless fabric of intimacy.

To say all of this is to recognize the irreplaceable role of the Virgin Mary, who stands at the very threshold by which God, in Christ, enters into our world. Indeed, we saw in week 2 that God, in his profound reverence for his creature, humbly seeks her permission in order to bestow himself upon her, and through her upon all of humanity. Mary is the Mother of Jesus, who receives him in obedience from God, brings him to birth, and nurtures and cares for him. However, her motherhood itself springs from a deeper attitude: from the attitude of a child and a spouse. In other words, her expansive fruitfulness, the radiant beauty of her transparency to God's light, is the expression of her innermost disposition of *contemplative receptivity* to God's Love and his gift. Because Mary knows herself to be loved, and cradled unceasingly in the arms of Love, she can confidently open her heart and her life (and her womb!) to welcome the gift of God, and to abandon herself trustingly to him in return. Her whole being, because of the pure grace of God which envelops her, is a total "Yes" to the Trinity. Through this "Yes," which simply echoes the loving "Yes" of God, she allows herself to be united to God in the most profound intimacy.

This "Yes" of Mary—which is an act of pure poverty, obedience, and chastity, the simple openness of loving trust—is what allows God, in and through her, to untie the knot of disobedience tied by Eve. And yet we said that this very untying of one knot—the knot that binds us to fear and sin, to pride, possessiveness, and lust—is possible only because another knot is tied, that of loving intimacy with God. In letting her whole being be "knitted together" into intimacy with her Son Jesus, and through him with the Father, Mary, in the name of all humanity, allows the threads of loving relationship to be re-tied. She is therefore truly the one who "in the single hearth of her love unites all the lines of contradiction." She is the Untier of Knots, but only because, in her complete childlike liberty, she helps liberate us too from sin and helps our hearts to be knitted together in love with the Heart of Jesus Christ.

Because of the unconditional openness of her consent to God's Love, Mary's heart is dilated to share in the very tenderness—in the very depth and breadth—of the Love of the Trinity. It is thus that, invited to be the Mother of Jesus, she also become the Mother of all humanity, as she stands in faith and love at the foot of the Cross. As we saw in week 4, Mary's "Yes" endures and matures throughout her life: as she surrenders ever more deeply to God's Mystery, which she discerns in every circumstance to be the Mystery of Love alone. She becomes thus truly the "ecclesial soul," who bears within her own heart the faith of all those who will come after her, reborn of water and the Holy Spirit. She is, in a real and profound way, the "Church-in-person," since she lives the central mystery of the Church as she takes her origin from the bosom of the Trinity, from the outpouring Love from the Heart of Christ.

To enter truly into the heartbeat of the Church, therefore, is to discover her "Marian mystery," to experience the enveloping love of the most tender Mother, who loves each one of us intimately and uniquely. We are opened, through experiencing the tender gaze of this Mother, to receive and experience the very loving gaze of God. In his gaze of love alone can we truly know who we are, our deepest identity as God's beloved. Yes, to enter into prayer is to open myself to this loving gaze of God—to let the gentle light cast from his eyes pour forth into all of the place of darkness and shame within me, but only so that he may touch the beauty deep inside me and set it free into the joy and confidence of love. Then, I come to experience, in those eyes, the ineffable Beauty of the One who looks upon me. His Beauty encounters my beauty, and the two are drawn together in a movement of mutual self-giving that blossoms in a profound and unbreakable intimacy.

Finally, from within this space of intimate loving encounter, my eyes are illumined to look upon every person within the radiance of God's own gaze, to see and to love them with the tenderness, compassion, and cherishing reverence with which God has first looked upon me. And Mary is here…Mary is here unceasingly, helping us to receive and to reciprocate this gaze of love, with God and with every person. It is she, in a special way, who helps us never to become lost in the "anonymous" crowd, but always draws out into the open the intimate depths of unique beauty in every person. It is thus that the true face—and the heart!—of the Church can become radiantly visible: intimate union with the Trinity, and, through the bond of the Trinity's Love, with every one of our brothers and sisters.

Reflection Question:

— *As I look back over these past weeks, what do I feel God has been most especially doing within me? How has he touched me, how has he loved me, how has he been inviting me deeper into his Love?*

DAY 33: HAND IN HER HAND, HEART IN HER HEART

We come at last to the end of our 33 days of preparation. Tomorrow we will make the act of complete entrustment into the hands and the heart of our heavenly Mother...and, through her, into the Heart of our loving God. Hopefully, however, this time has already been filled with innumerable little acts of entrustment, countless movements of prayer and love toward Mary, and especially toward God who reveals his love to us in and through her. The more "formal" act of entrustment or consecration which we are to make (or renew) is simply an expression of the growing relationship that already exists between us and Mary, between us and the Trinity—a relationship that endures even when we do not feel it.

We have seen that Mary, knowing herself to be constantly and completely loved by God, gave herself to him totally in simple childlike trust. And she yearns to take us by the hand and to help us make the same act of loving and childlike surrender—to place ourselves lovingly in the hands of the God who loves us. This is indeed her only desire: to facilitate the meeting between God and ourselves, to help us to receive the outpouring of his mercy into our whole being, especially where we need it the most, and to trustingly abandon ourselves into his hands in return.

The entrustment of ourselves to God through Mary, therefore, is simply our consent to allow her to do this—and to allow God to do it through her. Indeed, it is simply our recognition of God's Love, our grateful and faith-filled abandonment into the arms of this Love that already cradles us unceasingly. However imperfect we may feel our surrender to be, God receives it without hesitation—seeing our desire, our hope, and the innermost beauty of our heart—and, cradling us in himself, brings this surrender to perfection in complete intimacy with himself.

It is recommended that, today or tomorrow, you write your own personal "Entrustment to Mary" prayer—as an expression of the true desires and aspirations of your heart. There is a prayer provided below, however, which you may use. In either case, it is good to write it out in your own hand and, after praying it, to sign and date it. If it is possible to attend Mass and receive Communion tomorrow, then the thanksgiving after Communion is a beautiful and fitting time to make this formal act of total entrustment to Mary. But she is ever close to us, holding our hand within her hand, our heart within her heart, and so at any time and any place, she is there to receive this act of love and trust...

Yes, Mary, hold us tenderly, shelter us lovingly...and through your motherly presence, help us to know and to experience God's perfect Love. Let us know this Love which surpasses all comprehension—yet which is ever present to us, intimately cradling us, and in our certainty in this Love to abandon ourselves into his arms as a little child!

PRAYER OF ENTRUSTMENT TO MARY

Mary, pure and humble Virgin—Daughter, Bride, and Mother, united unceasingly to the Holy Trinity—I entrust myself entirely to you, in trust, gratitude, and simplicity. May I be a little child before you always—in your presence, in your arms, sheltered by your mantle and your love. Just as Jesus himself lived in your presence, both Son of Mary and Son of God, so may I also abide, Mary, at every moment, in the truth of childhood, cradled, close to you, in the arms of God's perfect Love.

I ask you to help me to gaze ever more deeply into the tender and loving gaze of God, who ceaselessly looks upon me and cries out: "You are my beloved, child, in whom I delight!" Yes, and through the radiance of this communication, may he live in me, and I in him. Dear Mary, form Jesus in me completely, just as he was formed in your heart and in your womb. And may I, in turn, let myself be ever more deeply and intimately cradled in his embrace. Bring to full flowering in me, healing all that hinders it, the fullness of his own mystery, and my own unique mystery in him, beautiful before the Father and before every person...this mystery that is already alive within my heart through God's gift.

Yes, grant me, through your motherly care, to rejoice to be a little, infinitely loved child of God. And with you, may this childhood blossom in the beauty of nuptial intimacy with Christ and of ever-deepening communion with my brothers and sisters. Finally, my Mother, grant me to radiate, in humble and joyful transparency, with the Father's own healing paternal light.

Fashion in me Jesus' own perfect humility, his filial intimacy with the Father, his own tender and reverent compassion for every person. And may you do this, Mary, by conforming me to your own virginal love, your own perfect acceptance and surrender of self, your own docility to the Spirit's slightest touch. It is thus that I will share, as you do, in the beauty of the love of God, bound together inseparably to the mystery of Christ who is the perfect Image of Divine Beauty.

Grant me to abide, dearest Mother, entirely within the enfolding arms of God, and thus to be, and to rejoice to be, one of the littlest and the least, utterly poor, utterly obedient, utterly chaste. In this little-ness, allow the gratuitous gift of God, passing through your virginal and maternal heart, to also pass into me, and through me into the hearts of others.

Touching all of us together, uniting us in the bosom of the holy Church, one Body and Bride of the Son, let this Love at last draw us into the inmost heart of Jesus' loving embrace, there to abide forever, with him, upon the Father's breast—in the intimacy and joy in which all things are made new, in the bliss of the Father, Son, and Holy Spirit, who live and reign forever and ever. Amen.

i. Henri de Lubac, *The Splendor of the Church*, trans. Michael Mason (San Francisco: Ignatius Press, 1999), 337-38. Quotations are from Paul Claudel, *L'Épée et le miroir*, 198-99.

ii. *Adversus Haereses*, III, 22, 4 (SC 211, 439-443.) Quoted in Denis Farkasfalvy, O.Cist., *The Marian Mystery: Outline of a Mariology* (New York: St. Paul's, 2014), 71-72.

iii. As quoted in the *Liturgy of the Hours* for the Memorial of St. Augustine, the second reading of the Office of Readings.